Mandela

FOR BEGINNERS

Tony Pinchuck

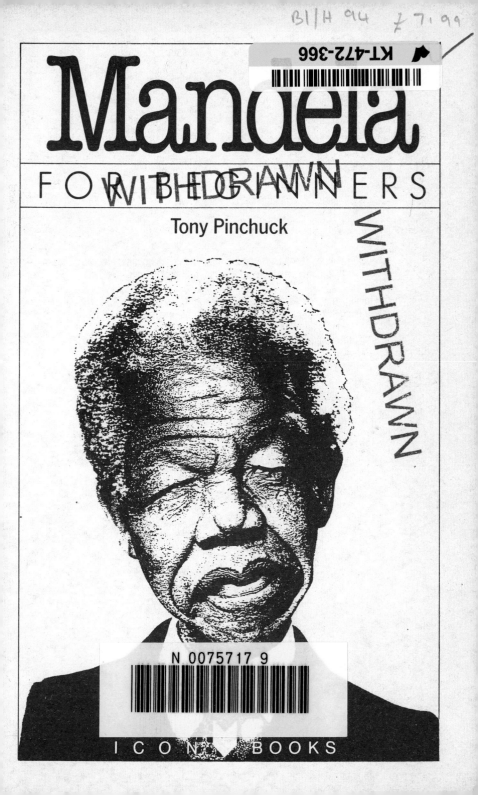

ICON BOOKS

Published in 1994 by Icon Books Ltd., Cavendish House,
Cambridge Road, Barton, Cambridge.

Published in Australia in 1994 by Allen & Unwin Pty, Ltd.,
PO Box 8500, 9 Atchison Street, St. Leonards, NSW 2065.

Text and illustrations copyright © 1994 Tony Pinchuck

A CIP catalogue record for this book is available from the British Library

ISBN 1 874166 22 6

Printed and bound in Great Britain by
The Bath Press, Avon

27 APRIL 1994
INANDA, NATAL

By the time he won the right to vote in his country's elections, Nelson Mandela was 76 years old. He had endured 27 years of imprisonment, preceded by decades of struggle. His release was followed by four years of bitter negotiations.

The poll in which he cast his ballot closed the world's chapter on institutionalized racism and conferred on Nelson Mandela the position of South Africa's first democratically elected president...

1918
QUNU

Nelson Mandela was born in 1918 at Qunu, near Umtata, the capital of the Transkei.

ROLIHLAHLA.

His second name, Rolihlahla, means "stirring up trouble" in Xhosa – his mother tongue.

MANDELA'S FIRST NAME SHOWS THE INFLUENCE OF EUROPE IN AFRICA – SOUTH AFRICA WAS PART OF THE BRITISH EMPIRE.

NELSON'S COLUMN TRAFALGAR SQUARE

Despite colonial influences, Nelson's upbringing was rooted in rural tradition. His father, Chief Hendry, was a member of the Thembu royal family. The Thembu are Xhosa speakers from South Africa's Transkei region.

Nelson's mother, Nosokeni Fanny, was the third of Chief Hendry's four wives. Nelson and his three sisters lived in their mother's kraal and shared her three huts.
He helped with herding the cattle and sheep and with ploughing.

In some respects his family lived in much the same way as their ancestors had for 20 generations before. But in other important ways things had changed dramatically. During the 300 years following the arrival of Europeans, Africans were gradually pushed from traditional lands and into increasingly smaller "reserves". By the time Nelson was born, Africans, who made up 78% of South Africa's population, had been squeezed into reserves that made up 7.3% of the land.

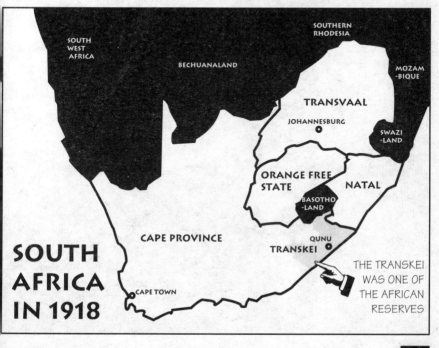

SOUTHERN RHODESIA

SOUTH WEST AFRICA

BECHUANALAND

MOZAM-BIQUE

TRANSVAAL

JOHANNESBURG

SWAZI-LAND

ORANGE FREE STATE

NATAL

BASOTHO-LAND

CAPE PROVINCE

QUNU

TRANSKEI

SOUTH AFRICA IN 1918

CAPE TOWN

THE TRANSKEI WAS ONE OF THE AFRICAN RESERVES

As a boy, Nelson listened to the elders' tales of his people in the days of their independence.

THEY SPOKE OF THE GOOD OLD DAYS BEFORE THE ARRIVAL OF THE WHITE MAN...

WE CONTROLLED OUR OWN ARMIES, AND ORGANIZED OUR OWN TRADE AND COMMERCE...

OUR PEOPLE LIVED PEACEFULLY UNDER THE DEMOCRATIC RULE OF THEIR KINGS AND COUNSELLORS AND MOVED FREELY ALL OVER THE COUNTRY...

THEN THE COUNTRY WAS OURS. WE OCCUPIED THE LAND, THE FORESTS AND RIVERS. WE SET UP AND OPERATED OUR OWN GOVERNMENT...

The first white settlers to land on South African soil arrived in 1652. They were members of the Dutch East India Company, which was engaged in trade between the Netherlands and Asia. Under the leadership of Jan van Riebeeck, their instructions were to set up a supply station at the Cape for their ships trading between Europe and the East.

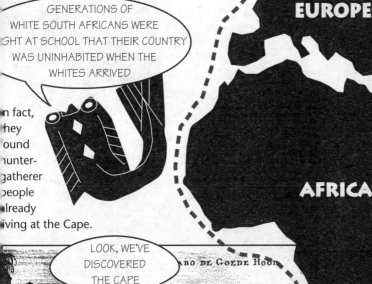

GENERATIONS OF WHITE SOUTH AFRICANS WERE ~~GHT~~ AT SCHOOL THAT THEIR COUNTRY WAS UNINHABITED WHEN THE WHITES ARRIVED

In fact, they found hunter-gatherer people already living at the Cape.

EUROPE

AFRICA

LOOK, WE'VE DISCOVERED THE CAPE

LOOK, I'VE DISCOVERED A BOATLOAD OF FOREIGNERS ON OUR BEACH.

CABO DE GOEDE HOOP

CAPE OF GOOD HOPE

Other parts of the country were inhabited by farming communities which raised crops, herded cattle and traded.

The newcomers didn't intend colonizing South Africa. They built a fort, grew vegetables and at first kept more or less to themselves. But they soon realized they needed labour to help with their farming. Van Riebeeck had very little success trying to recruit the local people.

One solution was to let some of the settlers become free burghers to run cattle ranches and farms which could supply produce to the Company. These "boers" (farmers) were given land around the fort which still stands in the centre of modern day Cape Town, but they soon spread further afield.

"The Khoikhoi strongly insisted that we had been appropriating more and more of their land, which had been theirs all these centuries and on which they had been accustomed to let their cattle graze.
They asked if they would be allowed to do such a thing if they went to Holland..."

(from the diary of Jan van Riebeeck)

Jan van Riebeeck

Van Riebeeck also introduced slaves, from West Africa and Dutch colonies in the East Indies. Slavery was the basis of agricultural production at the Cape till it was abolished in the 1830s.

In 1806 the British sailed in and took over the Cape.

THIS CAPE'S NOT SAFE WITH EMPIRE BUILDERS LIKE NAPOLEON ON THE LOOSE.

LET'S TAKE IT OVER FOR ITS OWN PROTECTION.

AYE AYE CAP'N – AND **AFTER** LUNCH?

In 1834 the British governor at the Cape abolished slavery.
Many Dutch settlers resented being told what to do by the English. One of their grievances was being forced to free their slaves. They left the colony to go into the hinterland beyond the grasp of Queen Victoria's government.

AFRIKANER MYTHOLOGY IS FULL OF THE HEROIC EXPLOITS OF THESE TREKBOERS.

THE EXTREMIST AWB (AFRIKANER RESISTANCE MOVEMENT) STILL DRAWS ON THIS BLOOD AND EARTH IMAGERY.

Meanwhile, elsewhere in South Africa, another massive movement of people had been unleashed. In the 1820s, the bastard son of the head of a small clan seized the chieftainship after his father's death.

HIS NAME WAS SHAKA... BUT HIS FRIENDS CALLED HIM "SIR".

Through a combination of ruthless tyranny and tactical brilliance Shaka created an awesome military force and turned his Zulu clan into one of the most powerful states in 19th century Africa. His military campaign, known as the *mfecane* (or crushing), sent shock waves through the subcontinent. Battle-weary tribes fled northwards as far as Tanzania and westwards into the Cape to escape.

THE MFECANE WAS ALSO KNOWN AS THE DIFAQANE– THE FORCED MIGRATIONS.

IT'S TO THIS PERIOD THAT ZULU NATIONALISTS LIKE CHIEF BUTHELEZI AND HIS INKATHA PARTY HARK BACK.

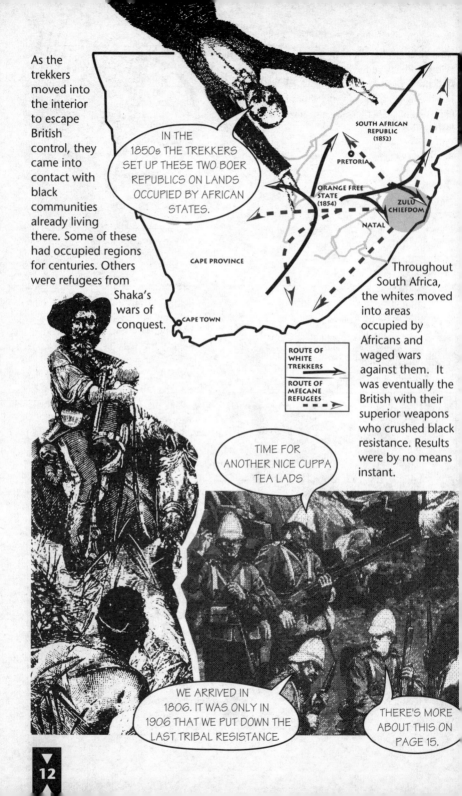

As the trekkers moved into the interior to escape British control, they came into contact with black communities already living there. Some of these had occupied regions for centuries. Others were refugees from Shaka's wars of conquest.

IN THE 1850s THE TREKKERS SET UP THESE TWO BOER REPUBLICS ON LANDS OCCUPIED BY AFRICAN STATES.

SOUTH AFRICAN REPUBLIC (1852)

PRETORIA

ORANGE FREE STATE (1854)

ZULU CHIEFDOM

NATAL

CAPE PROVINCE

CAPE TOWN

ROUTE OF WHITE TREKKERS

ROUTE OF MFECANE REFUGEES

Throughout South Africa, the whites moved into areas occupied by Africans and waged wars against them. It was eventually the British with their superior weapons who crushed black resistance. Results were by no means instant.

TIME FOR ANOTHER NICE CUPPA TEA LADS

WE ARRIVED IN 1806. IT WAS ONLY IN 1906 THAT WE PUT DOWN THE LAST TRIBAL RESISTANCE.

THERE'S MORE ABOUT THIS ON PAGE 15.

In 1860 South Africa's economy was based mainly on subsistence agriculture. The settlers had by this stage seized much of the fertile land. In both the British colonies of the Cape and Natal and the two Boer republics, whites relied extensively on the labour of Africans who were forced to live as tenants on land that had previously been their own. For the most part, the industrializing world showed little interest in this far off backwater.

SOUTH AFRICA – IS THAT SOMEWHERE ON THE OTHER SIDE OF THE THAMES, DARLING?

I HAVEN'T THE FOGGIEST, MY PET, IT ISN'T ON THIS MAP OF PLACES TO MAKE MONEY.

BUT THEN...

two very important discoveries changed all that.

1867

1886

GOLD!

DIAMONDS!

CHEERIO, MY DEARIO, I'M OFF TO SOUTH AFRICA.

These discoveries evoked considerable interest in Europe and especially Britain. Prospectors flocked to Kimberley for diamonds and the Witwatersrand region where gold was discovered. (This area is still often called "the Reef" after the enormous gold seams discovered there.)

Money for expensive mining equipment soon flowed in from foreign investors eager for big profits. (The West has always retained its strong link with the SA mines.) Although Africans had lost control of the country, many still lived by agriculture. They had no need to work in the mines. The government passed laws to compel them to supply their labour.

More and more people were forced off the land. This was the beginning of South Africa's migrant labour system. With much of the labour-force absent, crops got smaller and families poorer and less self-sufficient.

In 1906 the last period of struggle against white domination came to an end.
Africans in Natal became alarmed at their diminishing control over their own land.
In the early 1900s restrictions were placed on them buying land. Then a hefty
poll tax was imposed on adult males. Driven to desperation many refused to pay.
The authorities declared martial law and dealt ruthlessly with the resisters.

CHIEF BAMBATHA

WE WILL NOT
PAY TAXES TO A
FOREIGN GOVERNMENT!

BURN ALL
THEIR HUTS AND
POSSESSIONS AND TAKE
THEIR CATTLE.

This served to
inflame a full-
blown rebellion led
by Chief Bambatha.
He was joined by
Sigananda, chief of
the Cube.
Sigananda was by
this time very old.
As a boy he had
served as a mat
carrier in Shaka's
army.
The British
ruthlessly put
down the rebellion.
Four thousand
resistance fighters
were killed. Armed
struggle was ended
for the moment.

After the defeat of the Bambatha rebellion, the numbers of African men from Zululand working in the Transvaal shot up by 60 per cent. By 1909, 80 per cent of adult males in the territory were absent from their homes and working as migrant labourers. Migrant labour became an essential characteristic of South Africa's economic and social system. And later it became a basic cornerstone of apartheid.

AFTER THE REBELLION THE WHITES REALIZED THAT TOGETHER THEY WOULD BE STRONGER AGAINST THE BLACKS.

WHICH IS WHY IN 1910 THE BOER REPUBLICS AND BRITISH COLONIES JOINED IN THE UNION OF SOUTH AFRICA.

Migrant labour served two purposes from the government's point of view. The reserves weren't large enough to support the African population. Consequently they provided a ready supply of cheap labour. It was also hoped that, with their families in the rural areas, Africans would be only temporary residents in the white cities.

YOU DON'T HAVE TO PAY PROPER WAGES BECAUS THEIR FAMILIES IN THE RESERVE: SUPPORT THEM. THEIR PAY IS REALLY POCKET MONEY.

MY HUSBAND – NELSON'S FATHER – DIED. THERE'S NO MONEY TO SEND THE BOY TO SCHOOL.

I HAVE A LOT OF PRAISE FOR THIS INSTITUTION, BECAUSE IT IS PART OF ME, BUT ALSO DUE TO ITS USEFULNESS. IT CATERS FOR EVERYONE DESCENDED FROM A SINGLE ANCESTOR AND HOLDS THEM TOGETHER AS A FAMILY.

BUT TODAY THE FLOCKING OF PEOPLE TO THE CITIES, MINES AND FARMS MAKES IT DIFFICULT FOR THE INSTITUTION TO FUNCTION.

Nelson was just ten. His mother was poor and illiterate. But before his father's death, his parents had decided that their son would get an education. He was sent to live with the acting paramount chief of his tribe, the Thembu. As was the custom, Nelson became the chief's son. The man took this responsibility seriously.

Nelson shared a hut with the chief's son, Justice. They became close friends. The chief gave Nelson the western education his parents had wanted for him. When he completed primary school there was a huge celebration. It was a big event and a goat was slaughtered. Because there was no local high school the young Mandela became a boarder at Healdtown High School.

At 16, Nelson went to circumcision lodge on the banks of the Bashee River. This rite of passage made him a man within his tribe.

AFTER WEEKS CAMPING IN THE WILD AWAY FROM THE REST OF THE COMMUNITY, WE CAN JOIN THE MEN IN MAKING DECISIONS.

At this time Nelson became interested in the law. During school holidays he would spend time watching his guardian conduct tribal court cases. He enjoyed observing the way in which each side would present its case and the chief would then pass judgement.

I OBJECT TO THAT LINE OF CROSS-EXAMINATION M'LUD...

I SUBMIT THAT THE ACCUSED WAS NOWHERE NEAR THE SCENE OF THE CRIME...

Nelson matriculated from Healdtown in 1938, and the following year he went to Fort Hare University College. Started by missionaries, Fort Hare was one of the first serious educational institutions for blacks. Based on liberal values, it educated a number of Southern African leaders including Robert Mugabe of Zimbabwe and Sir Seretse Khama of Botswana, both of whom led their countries to independence. Nelson began a BA degree there, met Oliver Tambo and spent time sneaking out of his dormitory at night with his nephew Kaiser Matanzima to go ballroom dancing.

1939
FORT HARE

NELSON WAS SENSITIVE AND HATED BEING PATRONIZED. BUT HE WAS ALWAYS POPULAR.

OLIVER REGINALD TAMBO

Born in Bizana in the Transkei in 1917, Tambo was the son of peasant farmers. His early brilliance at a local mission school and then at St Peter's in Johannesburg earned him a scholarship to Fort Hare in 1938. He went on to become ANC president (until replaced by Mandela in 1991) and then chairman, until his death in April 1993.

In his third year of studies Nelson became involved in a boycott of classes in protest at the hostel food at Fort Hare. The authorities expelled the organizers. Nelson was sent home. The boycotters were given an ultimatum.

STOP THE BOYCOTT OR STAY AWAY...

...PERMANENTLY!

Nelson was about to abandon the protest and return to Fort Hare.

WHEN...

MY GUARDIAN FELT IT WAS TIME FOR ME TO GET MARRIED. HE LOVED ME VERY MUCH AND LOOKED AFTER ME AS DILIGENTLY AS MY FATHER HAD. BUT HE WAS NO DEMOCRAT AND DID NOT THINK IT WORTHWHILE TO CONSULT ME. ABOUT A WIFE.

HE SELECTED A GIRL, FAT AND DIGNIFIED; **LOBOLA*** WAS PAID AND ARRANGEMENTS WERE MADE FOR THE WEDDING.

*LOBOLA = BRIDE PRICE, TRADITIONALLY PAID IN CATTLE

Nelson ran away to Johannesburg with his old pal, Justice. It was an epic journey that took them across South Africa. They went by bus through the Eastern Cape, catching the train for Johannesburg in Natal.

WE'RE OFF TO EGOLI – THE CITY OF GOLD.

NELSON'S REJECTION OF AN ARRANGED MARRIAGE REPRESENTED A MORE FUNDAMENTAL REJECTION OF STRAIGHTFORWARD TRADITION..

I WANT TO BE PART OF SOUTH AFRICA'S FUTURE...

Nelson and Justice were part of a massive black migration, in the 1940s, that took thousands of men from the impoverished rural areas throughout Southern Africa to seek work in the region's industrial powerhouse – Johannesburg. Huge mine-dumps on the outskirts of the city centre still reflect its origins in the late 19th century – in goldmining.

In the 1940s South Africa experienced accelerated economic growth. A faraway war in Europe was having its enormous impact. Gold and other minerals had fuelled the country's first industrial revolution. But now a second – in manufacturing – was under way. Britain's resources were being diverted away from consumer manufacturing and into its war effort. Not only was South African industry making a contribution to the allied forces, but it could no longer rely on imports. It needed to make its own goods. This spurred the growth of a broad manufacturing base. Johannesburg was at the centre of these developments.

AFRICAN CONSCRIPTS JOINED THE ALLIED WAR EFFORT. BUT THE GOVERNMENT WAS AFRAID TO GIVE US GUNS.

Nelson discovered an urban life that was fast, lively and influenced by the United States. Gangster movies, American writers and singers became part of township culture as did jazz...

THE JAZZ MANIACS WERE ONE OF THE MOST POPULAR SWING BANDS OF THE 1930s & 1940s.

THEY PLAYED FOR THE ARMED FORCES DURING WORLD WAR II AND BECAME KNOWN AS "THE JAZZ FORCES".

South Africa had something else in common with the United States...

...SEGREGATION!

THE WINTERS IN JOHANNESBURG CAN BE BITTERLY COLD.

Many facilities such as libraries were not open to blacks. Certain skilled jobs were by law restricted to whites. But it was most harshly felt in living conditions. Blacks who flocked to the cities found that their numbers far outstripped housing provision. Africans often defied the government and set up shanty towns using flimsy materials like sacking or old paraffin cans.

EVEN FIREWOOD HAS GONE TO WAR!

23

In Johannesburg, Nelson and Justice knew just one person. He was an old induna (captain) of the Chief. The man was honoured to host members of the royal family and provided the two with somewhere to stay.

He helped Nelson to get a job at Crown Mines as a policeman guarding the men-only hostels.

CROWN MINES

> HERE'S YOUR UNIFORM & KNOBKERRIE*. IF YOU'RE GOOD YOU'LL GET PROMOTED TO CLERK.

But within days...

*STAVE

... an envoy from the paramount chief had tracked Nelson down.

> COME HOME NOW!

> I WANT TO BE A LAWYER.

Walter Sisulu ran his small estate agency from central Jo'burg. He sold property in those few areas of the city where blacks were allowed to own freehold.

WALTER MAX ULYATE SISULU

Born in Engcobo in the Transkei in 1912, Sisulu came to Johannesburg where he held down a succession of jobs. He first worked in a dairy, then a mile below ground digging for gold at the rock face. He was also a kitchen hand in a white household, followed by a series of jobs in factories. At the same time he studied by correspondence. In 1940 he joined the ANC, becoming its secretary general in 1949. When Mandela walked into his office in 1941 Sisulu was living with his mother who took in washing for white families.

HOW ABOUT A NICE LITTLE COTTAGE (CORRUGATED IRON SHACK), BEAUTIFUL LOCATION (NEXT TO THE GARBAGE DUMP), NEEDS SOME DECORATION (FALLING APART)?

Nelson explained his situation and Walter immediately offered him a job. He also invited Nelson to stay with him at his mother's house. He helped pay Nelson's fees to study for a BA degree by correspondence and ...

...found him a wife.
Evelyn Ntoko Mase was a nurse at City Deep Mine Hospital.

WITHIN DAYS OF OUR FIRST MEETING, WE WERE GOING STEADY AND WITHIN MONTHS HE PROPOSED.

WITHIN A YEAR I WAS EXPECTING OUR FIRST CHILD. WE WERE VERY EXCITED, AND NELSON'S JOY WAS THERE FOR ALL TO SEE WHEN THEMBI WAS BORN.

IN 1947 WE MOVED TO A THREE-ROOMED MATCHBOX HOUSE NO 8115 IN ORLANDO WEST.

Nelson and Evelyn had four children. Their son, Thembi, died while Nelson was on Robben Island. A daughter was born in 1948 but lived only nine months. In 1950 they had their second son Makgatho; and their eldest surviving daughter, Makaziwe, was born in 1954.

1942
WITS
UNIVERSITY

Nelson completed his BA degree and enrolled part time for a law degree at Witwatersrand University in Johannesburg. While there he was articled to a firm of white lawyers.

HERE HE SHOWED EARLY EVIDENCE OF DIPLOMACY...

ON MY FIRST DAY AT THE OFFICE, THE WHITE SENIOR TYPIST SAID...

LOOK, NELSON, WE HAVE NO COLOUR BAR HERE. WHEN THE TEA BOY BRINGS THE TEA COME AND GET YOURS FROM THE TRAY. WE'VE BOUGHT TWO NEW CUPS FOR YOU AND GAUR RADIKE. YOU MUST USE THEM. TELL GAUR ABOUT THE CUPS. BE CAREFUL OF HIM, NELSON. HE'S A BAD INFLUENCE.

WHEN I TOLD GAUR (ANOTHER AFRICAN EMPLOYEE), HIS RESPONSE WAS: "I'LL SHOW YOU. DO EXACTLY AS I DO." WHEN THE TEA ARRIVED, GAUR BOYCOTTED THE NEW CUPS AND PICKED ONE OF THE OLD ONES.

I HAD NO DESIRE TO QUARREL WITH HIM OR THE SENIOR TYPIST, SO FOR MONTHS I DID NOT DRINK TEA.

On the campus Nelson made contact with people of all races and political views. In the 1940s, South Africa's universities were not yet rigidly segregated, and bannings had not stifled political debate (as they were going to in the 1950s). He came across Africanism, liberalism and Marxism. His fellow law students, Ismail Meer and JN Singh, were members of the Natal Indian Congress which was about to become engaged in passive resistance against the "Ghetto Act", a new Land Act, which would segregate Indians.

He met white communists, including Ruth First and her husband Joe Slovo as well as Bram Fischer.
The Communist Party was the most effective at organizing, particularly among black workers.

I WONDER HOW THEY DO IT.

Initially he was drawn to Africanism – the idea of forging an African nation. This raised some awkward questions in his mind about multiracialism...

NELSON WAS A KEEN AMATEUR BOXER.

AFRICANISM TAKES US FORWARD FROM TRIBALISM TO THE AFRICAN NATION. BUT HOW DO WHITES, INDIANS AND COLOUREDS FIT INTO THIS NATION?

For one such Africanist, Anton Lembede, who was an influence on the young Mandela, the answer was... simple...

Ironically, Lembede developed his ideas by reading *Die Transvaler*, a pro-fascist, anti-semitic and anti-British newspaper edited by a certain Dr Verwoerd – the high priest of apartheid, in fact.

THEY DON'T !

VERWOERD IS SINGLE-MINDED ON BEHALF OF AFRIKANERS. AFRICANS NEED AN EQUALLY SINGLE-MINDED PHILOSOPHY.

AFRICA IS THE BLACK MAN'S COUNTRY. WE HAVE INHABITED AFRICA, OUR MOTHERLAND, FROM TIME IMMEMORIAL; AFRICA BELONGS TO US!

Nelson was at first inspired by these radical ideas, which drew him into the ANC. Dissatisfaction with the leadership was growing. He became one of a group of restive young men who wanted to galvanise the organisation and challenge an old guard they felt had failed to attack white domination.

1944
THE ANC

I THOUGHT THE ANC WAS A RADICAL PARTY – NOT A GENTS' CLUB. HOW DID IT RUN OUT OF STEAM?

The ANC – African National Congress – had been formed some 32 years previously, in 1912. The founders were mission-educated members of the African middle class, with no intention of overthrowing the white government. They simply wanted recognition by white society and took the words of Cecil John Rhodes – *equal rights for all civilized men* – at face value.

CECIL RHODES WAS THE ARCH COLONIALIST. HE OWNED MINES IN THE TRANSVAAL & WAS PRIME MINISTER OF THE CAPE. HE BELIEVED RELIGIOUSLY IN THE BRITISH EMPIRE AND WANTED TO MAKE AFRICA BRITISH.

RHODESIA (ZIMBABWE) WAS COLONIZED BY HIS PRIVATE COMPANY AND THE COUNTRY NAMED AFTER HIM.

Middle class blacks already enjoyed the vote in the Cape Province on the basis of a qualified franchise. The early ANC leaders simply wanted this to be extended to the rest of the country. Later, they hoped, the vote would be granted to all the masses. They saw as their model the evolutionary growth of democracy in Britain.

Sol Plaatje

S Msane

Rev J L Dube (first ANC president)

T Mapileka

Dr W Rubusana

In 1914 the ANC's leaders went as a deputation to London to protest against the 1913 Land Act, which severely restricted property ownership by blacks.
The trip was unsuccessful.

COME AND HEAR
Mr. SOL
PLAATJE
Of Kimberley, South Africa

Gives thrilling account of the condition of the Colored Folk in British South Africa.

A Touching Message well and truly ...

The story has gripped nearly a thousand audiences in England, Scotland, Canada & U.S.

IT WILL THRILL YO...

Bethel A. M. E. Church
West 132nd Street, bet. Lenox and 5th Aves.

Sunday, March 13, 11 a. m.
THE BLACK MAN'S BURDEN IN SOUTH AFRICA

Friday, March 18th, 8 p. m.
THE BLACK WOMAN'S BURDEN IN SO. AFRICA
Interspersed with Quaint African Music sung in his own native tongue

Free Will Offering for Brotherhood Work among the South African Tribes

ADMISSION FREE
COME EARLY AND AVOID THE CRUSH !!
DR. MONTROSE W. THORNTON, Pastor

SORRY YOU BLACK CHAPPIES, BUT WE'VE GOT A WHITE MAN'S WAR ON HERE – JUST HAVEN'T THE TIME.

Growing frustration with the inadequacy of the ANC as an effective mass organization led to the rise of a number of alternatives.

THE ANC LEADERS ARE GOOD BOYS TIED TO THE APRON STRINGS OF THE WHITE LIBERALS.

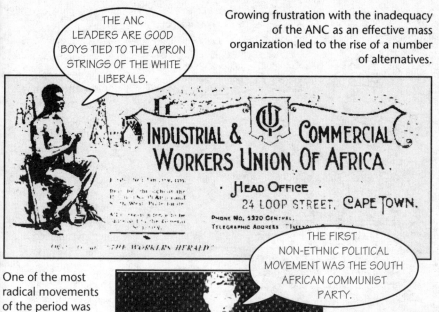

INDUSTRIAL & COMMERCIAL WORKERS UNION OF AFRICA.

· HEAD OFFICE ·
24 LOOP STREET, CAPE TOWN.
PHONE No. 5320 CENTRAL.
TELEGRAPHIC ADDRESS "INDUSTRIAL"

"THE WORKERS HERALD"

THE FIRST NON-ETHNIC POLITICAL MOVEMENT WAS THE SOUTH AFRICAN COMMUNIST PARTY.

One of the most radical movements of the period was the Industrial and Commercial Workers Union founded in 1919. At its peak in 1928 it had gathered an impressive 150,000 members, but it petered out in the 1930s.

Formed in 1921 the SACP had a multiracial executive. While it never gained wide membership it exerted an influence on the ANC in the post-war period.

Stanley Silwana

John Gomas

T Mapileka

ONE OF THE MORE BIZARRE MOVEMENTS TO ARISE FROM AFRICAN FRUSTRATION WAS THE TRANSKEI BASED CULT WHICH PUT ITS FAITH IN AMA MELIKA...

...THEY BELIEVED THAT BLACK AMERICANS WERE COMING IN SHIPS AND PLANES TO FREE THEM AND WIPE OUT WHITES AND NON-BELIEVERS.

The ANC leadership, dominated by middle class professionals, on the other hand, put their faith in petitions, pleas and speeches. These proved just as fruitless. They achieved no major victories for black rights.

In fact in 1936, they suffered a serious setback, when the government terminated the franchise for Africans in the Cape. The ANC sent a deputation to prime minister Hertzog to protest.

HERTZOG TREATED THE DELEGATION VERY BADLY. THEY WERE NOT EVEN GIVEN SEAT AND THE SITUATION WAS SUCH TH THE LEADER OF THE GROUP DIDN' EVEN HAVE THE COURAGE TO LOOK AT HERTZOG.

HERTZOG JUST SAID: "WELL YOU'VE SEEN THE NEWSPAPERS." AFTER THAT THE ANC WAS SEEN AS BEING WEAK.

Led by Lembede, a group of "young Turks", including Mandela, Tambo and Sisulu formed the Youth League. They put forward radical tactics that would shift the ANC from polite pleas to mass action. They were against working with other organizations such as the Indian Congress.

1944
ANC YOUTH LEAGUE

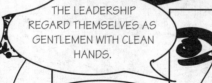

IT'S TRUE THAT THE ANC PROVIDES AFRICANS WITH A UNITED FRONT AGAINST OPPRESSION, BUT IT'S ORGANIZATIONALLY WEAK.

THE LEADERSHIP REGARD THEMSELVES AS GENTLEMEN WITH CLEAN HANDS.

WE NEED AUTHENTIC AFRICAN PHILOSOPHIES. WE MUST REJECT THE WHOLESALE IMPORTATION OF FOREIGN IDEOLOGIES.

In 1944 Lembede was elected president of the League. Although its founding manifesto criticized the ANC leadership, it also acknowledged their past efforts in promoting African rights.

OUR FATHERS FOUGHT SO THAT WE, BETTER EQUIPPED WHEN OUR TIME CAME, SHOULD START WHERE THEY STOPPED.

1945
EUROPE

The defeat of tyranny in Europe brought hopes that the South African government would now move away from segregation and begin to grant the dis-enfranchised majority their rights.

COSMETICS By MARION
STUTTAFORDS

Cape ✦ **Times**
VICTORY EDITION
TUESDAY, MAY 8, 1945

FOR LONGER EVENINGS
STUTTAFORDS

VE-DAY: END OF WAR IN EUROPE
Formal Announcement To-day

Surrender Signed at Eisenhower's H.Q.

10,000,000 GERMANS NOW PRISONERS

THE UNCONDITIONAL
German fighting for...
Count Schwerin...
Radio...

Statement by Mr. Hofmeyr To-day

To-morrow will be a Public Holiday

Military Chief to Broadcast

> I ENJOYED THAT. HOW WAS IT FOR YOU?

TO-DAY IS VE-DAY

Timetable

to-night.

BIG U-BOAT FLEET

The King Thanks Allied Expeditionary Forces

Victory Broadcast to Canada

To-day's Weath...

Eisenhower's Tribute to Britain

VE-Day Holiday Request

It soon became obvious that the government was not about to make any far-reaching concessions to black demands despite murmurs of change elsewhere in Africa. White control began to loosen in the rest of the continent. In the decades after the war the European powers conceded independence to most of their colonies.

But in South Africa the grip of minority control was about to tighten.

In this mood of heightened frustration even conservative African leaders lost patience. Councillor Paul Mosaka complained...

WE HAVE BEEN ASKED TO CO-OPERATE WITH A TOY TELEPHONE. WE HAVE BEEN SPEAKING INTO AN APPARATUS WHICH CANNOT TRANSMIT SOUND.

Congress Series No. 11.

AFRICANS' CLAIMS

IN SOUTH AFRICA.

Issued and Published by the African National Congress, Rosenberg Arcade, 58, Market Street, Johannesburg, and Printed by the Liberty Printers, 125, 6th Street, Asiatic Bazaar, Pretoria.

The 1945 annual conference of the ANC adopted a document that reflected an emerging politicization resulting from the experience of the second world war and particularly the defeat of nazism. The document called for universal franchise and an end to the colour bar, which restricted certain skilled jobs to whites.

37

1946
MINERS' STRIKE

The war years were a period of industrial militancy. Despite government bans on worker action, between 1942 and 1944 there were 60 strikes. The end of the second world war brought hopes that living standards would stop falling. These hopes proved empty, and in August 1946 the African Mineworkers Union launched a massive strike. Virtually the entire Witwatersrand gold-mining region came to a standstill as 100,000 workers stopped work. It was one of the largest displays of mass action in South Africa up to that time.

Prime minister Jan Smuts sent in the police who surrounded the miners compounds and forced the workers back down the shafts at gunpoint. In one incident police opened fire, killing nine and injuring 1,248

WELL, GUNS WORKED IN THE SECOND WORLD WAR, WHEN WE WERE FIGHTING ALONGSIDE THE ALLIES AGAINST THE NAZIS.

WAS THIS BY ANY CHANCE THE SAME GENERAL JAN SMUTS WHO WROTE THE PREAMBLE TO THE U N CHARTER ON HUMAN RIGHTS?

One and the same. General Smuts also has a statue to his memory outside Britain's parliament. Despite his denial of human rights to his fellow countrymen, he was well loved by the British for fighting alongside them for freedom and democracy in two world wars.

MEANWHILE...

At the United Nations, Dr Xuma, president of the ANC, condemned the Smuts government for its heavy handed approach to the issues facing South Africa.

WHEN WE ASK FOR BREAD WE GET LEAD!

ALFRED BITINI XUMA

Born in the Transkei in 1893 to an aristocratic family, Xuma saved sufficient funds to travel to the United States. There he worked his way through college and went on to get a medical degree in Europe before returning to South Africa. He was elected ANC president in 1940, when the organization had hit an all-time low. He worked through the 1940s trying to revitalize it and by revising its constitution and forging an alliance with the Natal Indian Congress.

In 1947, the ANC Youth League was thrown into mourning and confusion when the inspirational Anton Lembede unexpectedly died. Nelson was with him at lunchtime when Lembede suffered an intestinal problem. He was rushed to hospital and by the evening he was gone.

A P Mda succeeded him as Youth League president...

and Nelson took his first step into public life when he was voted general secretary.

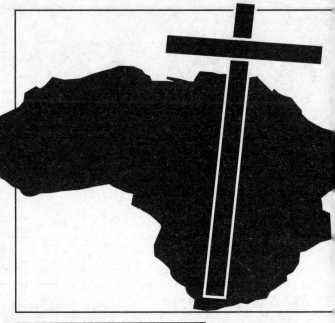

NELSON **WHO?**

Domestic and international pressures were bearing down on the Smuts government. The process of European decolonization began in earnest when Britain withdrew from India in 1947. This appeared to have implications for South Africa's blacks. But more important was the relentless influx into the country's urban areas. The traditional stereotype of Africans as rural tribespeople no longer conformed to reality. South Africa had a growing urban African population that wasn't about to go away.

IT WAS A CONFUSING TIME BUT IT WAS ALSO EXCITING.

SO WHAT DID THE GOVERNMENT DO?

The government did what governments always do when faced with a problem. It appointed a commission – to examine the Pass Laws.

The Pass Laws were the fundamental instruments of apartheid. Every African over 16 outside the bantustans had to carry a passbook. The main aim of the Pass Law system was to ensure that only Africans who had jobs could come into the white-designated areas of South Africa. This meant that millions of Africans were condemned to a ghettoized existence in the rural areas, where there was rarely any work, poverty reigned and infant mortality was high. The Pass Laws essentially treated Africans as foreigners in their own country.

WHAT WERE THESE PASS LAWS?

THEY USED THE DOMPAS TO MAKE SURE OUR LABOUR WAS WHERE THEY WANTED IT....

...AND NOWHERE ELSE.

For years the government had hinted at easing up on segregation. Even prime minister Smuts, who was no soft liberal, had suggested that it would probably have to end. His deputy, J H Hofmeyr, had thrown caution to the winds and staked his reputation on scrapping legislation that restricted skilled jobs to whites, and effectively maintained blacks as an economic underclass.

SEGREGATION HAS FALLEN ON EVIL DAYS!

I TAKE MY STAND ON THE ULTIMATE REMOVAL OF THE COLOUR BAR.

So when the Fagan Commission reported its findings in 1948, there was little surprise...

THE TREND TO URBANIZATION IS IRREVERSIBLE. PASS LAWS SHOULD BE EASED.

While some blacks may have felt heartened by this sign of reform, for many whites it was quite the last thing they wanted to hear...

For Afrikaners, the threat seemed especially acute. It raised all sorts of fears about being swamped by blacks, having their jobs taken by cheaper African workers and their identity becoming diluted...

Against this background of black aspiration and white fear, the Smuts government called an election. The opposition National Party campaigned on a "swart gevaar" (black peril) ticket, which pandered to every white fear.

WE'LL SOLVE EVERYONE'S PROBLEMS (AS LONG AS THEY'RE WHITE).

They promised to satisfy a variety of conflicting demands – no matter how contradictory.

AND ON THE OTHER HAND WE'LL BRING THEM TO THE CITIES PLENTIFUL SUPPLY OF CHE LABOUR.

ON THE ONE HAND WE'LL SEND THE BLACKS BACK TO THEIR RESERVES...

The tactic worked. The Nationalists won the election, defeating Smuts' United Party by a narrow margin.

On Friday 28 May Nelson Mandela and the ANC woke up to the nightmare reality of a National Party victory.
The party's leader, Daniel F Malan, was summoned by the governor general to form a cabinet.
On 1 June, he arrived by train at the administrative capital, Pretoria, where he addressed a group of supporters.

FOR THE FIRST TIME SOUTH AFRICA IS OUR OWN. MAY GOD GRANT THAT IT ALWAYS REMAINS OUR OWN.

IN THE PAST WE FELT LIKE STRANGERS IN OUR OWN LAND, BUT TODAY IT BELONGS TO US ONCE MORE.

NET BLANKES
WHITES ONLY

There are roughly 4.5 million whites in South Africa, made up of around 45% English speakers, largely of British descent and 55% Afrikaners, predominantly of Dutch descent (with some French and German input).

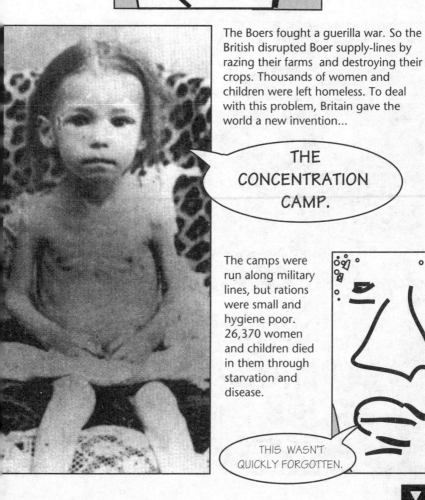

REMEMBER, ALSO, HOW MINERALS WERE DISCOVERED IN THE BOER 'UBLICS IN 1886? WELL, SUDDENLY THE BRITS TOOK AN INTEREST.

Britain declared war on the Boers in 1899, but it was no pushover. The greatest empire on earth had already suffered an ignominious defeat against the Boers in 1881. This time, the British were determined to win.

The Boers fought a guerilla war. So the British disrupted Boer supply-lines by razing their farms and destroying their crops. Thousands of women and children were left homeless. To deal with this problem, Britain gave the world a new invention...

THE CONCENTRATION CAMP.

The camps were run along military lines, but rations were small and hygiene poor. 26,370 women and children died in them through starvation and disease.

THIS WASN'T QUICKLY FORGOTTEN.

During the first half of the 20th century, large numbers of Afrikaners were forced to leave the rural areas. This was partly a result of the Boer war, but also through overcrowding, drought and pestilence.

THE MINES, BANKS AND OTHER COMMANDING HEIGH OF THE ECONOMY WERE CONTROLLED BY ENGLISH – SPEAKERS.

As blacks were to do in the 1940s, these white dispossessed flocked to the towns looking for work.

MANY AFRIKANERS BECAME PART OF AN IMPOVERISHED WHITE WORKING CLASS.

HELP THE MAYOR'S SOUP KITCHEN FUND

And as their black counterparts were to do in 1946, white miners went on strike in 1922. And they too were dealt with by prime minister Smuts' army. Aircraft were sent in to bomb the towns of Benoni and Germiston.

WE WERE HOUNDED BY THE ENGLISH CAPITALISTS AN THE BLACKS WERE AFTER OUR JOBS.

1918
TWO BIRTHDAYS

WE HAD 1918 ALREADY WHEN NELSON MANDELA WAS BORN DIDN'T WE?

THERE WAS ANOTHER BIRTHDAY WHEN THIS LOT GOT TOGETHER IN 1918.

FEELING BROODY BROEDERS? HOW ABOUT GIVING BIRTH TO A BOND?

In 1918 a group of Afrikaners formed the Broederbond (brotherhood) to promote the interests of Afrikaners and to forge an Afrikaner nation in South Africa.
It aimed to uplift impoverished members of the volk (people) and to develop a sense of pride in their language, religion and culture.
Ultimately the Broederbond would come to influence every aspect of the way the country was run for close on half a century.

1930s
GERMANY

During the 1930s many bright young Afrikaners went to Europe to study. They found inspiration there in fascism, which was on the move in Spain, Italy, Portugal and, notably, Germany. In the extreme forms of nationalism they encountered, they believed they had found a philosophy that would carry forward their own people.

It was during this same period that Afrikaner intellectuals began to use the term **Apartheid**.

THAT'S PRONOUNCED: **APART HATE.** IT MEANS SEPARATENESS.

Among those who studied in Germany in the 1930s were Nico Diederichs, who became minister of finance under the National Party government; Hendrik Verwoerd, who was prime minister of South Africa from 1958 to 1966; and Piet Meyer, who was controller of the state broadcasting service for 20 years.

Piet Meyer called his son...

1938

Nico Diederichs, who later became chairman of the Broederbond, formed the Reddingsdaadbond (the Rescue Action League) in 1938, with the aim of kickstarting the Afrikaner economy by investing in exclusively Afrikaner enterprises. Between 1939 and 1949, it helped to launch 10,000 Afrikaner businesses. Some were small, but others grew to become major players in the South African economy.

THIS IS A JOB FOR SUPERBROEDER.

They include the multinational Rembrandt Tobacco, Volkskas (the country's third largest bank), Sanlam insurance company, Saambou building society and Gencor (one of South Africa's top five mining houses).

The Second World War split Afrikanerdom. There were those like Prime Minister Smuts who firmly stood in favour of joining the War alongside Britain. But for others, like John Vorster, Britain was the old enemy, and they supported Germany.

Some joined the Ossewa Brandwag (Ox Wagon Torch Commando) which carried out sabotage against the government. Hendrik van den Bergh, who later became head of BOSS* – the political police – was one. So was John Vorster.

*Bureau of State Security

BALTHAZAR JOHN VORSTER

Born in 1915, Vorster was a lawyer by training. He was jailed by Smuts during the war for sabotage. After hostilities ended, he applied to join the Nationalist Party – but was rejected for being too authoritarian in outlook. Little over a decade later he was in the National government cabinet. In 1966 he became prime minister of South Africa.

1948
REVISITED

The arrival of the
National Party
train at Pretoria
coincided with a
radical departure
for the
ANC.

IF WE STILL
BELIEVED IN PRAYERS,
PLEAS AND DEPUTATIONS,
THEN PRIME MINISTER
MALAN PUT AN   END TO
THAT.

WE AFRIKANERS ARE
NOT THE WORK OF MAN, BUT A
CREATION OF GOD. IT IS TO US THAT
MILLIONS OF SEMI-BARBAROUS BLACKS LOOK
FOR GUIDANCE, JUSTICE AND THE
CHRISTIAN WAY OF LIFE.

D F MALAN
PRIME MINISTER

The December 1949 ANC annual conference in Bloemfontein was stormy. Deep splits appeared between the Youth League and the old guard. The League favoured a more active approach to opposing the government.

NEW TACTICS ARE NEEDED TO COMBAT THIS NEW GOVERNMENT...

...OTHERWISE IT'LL ALL END IN SPEECHES

ALTHOUGH THE '46 MINERS' STRIKE ENDED IN FAILURE, IT SHOWED THAT THE MASSES CAN BE ORGANIZED.

The League put forward its historic **Programme of Action** to the conference. It demanded that the ANC refuse to collaborate with structures provided by the government for blacks.

It was agreed that Tambo and Sisulu would approach Xuma before the conference and give him an ultimatum...

At the eleventh hour, the Youth Leaguers were forced to search for a suitable replacement for Xuma. They settled on Dr James Moroka. By this time they had majority support and got their man elected.

DR JAMES MOROKA
ANC PRESIDENT 1949-52

Walter Sisulu was elected secretary general. Nelson Mandela was voted onto the ANC executive, and the Programme of Action was adopted.

And Nelson explained the tactics to the meeting...

OUR ARSENAL WILL INCLUDE NEW WEAPONS: BOYCOTT, STRIKE, CIVIL DISOBEDIENCE AND NON-CO-OPERATION.

DR MOROKA WAS BARELY SUITABLE, BUT HE WAS "OUR" PRESIDENT. WE ELECTED A FIRST RATE SECRETARY IN WALTER SISULU.

A P MDA WAS THE FIREBRAND AMONG THE YOUTH. WE WERE ALL AFRICANISTS, BUT TO DIFFERENT DEGREES. NELSON WAS TO MY RIGHT, CLOSER TO MDA. TAMBO, I COULD NEVER LAY MY FINGER ON. HE WAS THE PERFECT DIPLOMAT. HE AND NELSON HAD A WAY OF HIDING THEIR FEELINGS.

DILIZA MJI
YOUTH LEAGUER

1950
MAY DAY

HAVE YOU HEARD THIS? THE COMMUNISTS, THE INDIAN CONGRESS AND THE TRANSVAAL ANC ARE CALLING A NATIONAL STOPPAGE FOR MAY DAY.

!!!!

Nelson and the Youth Leaguers were furious. They opposed co-operation with non-African groups. And they had got Moroka elected precisely to avoid it. They lambasted the May Day organizers, broke up their meetings and attacked communism.

AFRICANS ARE OPPRESSED PRIMARILY AS BLACKS AND ONLY SECONDARILY AS WORKERS...

THE EXOTIC PLANT OF COMMUNISM CANNOT FLOURISH ON AFRICAN SOIL.

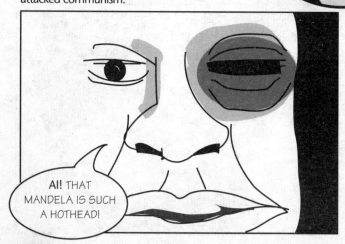

AI! THAT MANDELA IS SUCH A HOTHEAD!

May Day came. Against all the odds, the strike was a great success with half the workforce staying away – despite Youth League opposition, a government ban on public meetings and the presence of 2,000 armed police.

However, it ended in bloodshed, when police attacked meetings. Nineteen Africans were killed and 30 wounded. But it provided a graphic lesson to Nelson.

THAT DAY WAS A TURNING POINT IN MY LIFE...

I GOT FIRST HAND EXPERIENCE OF THE RUTHLESSNESS OF THE POLICE...

AND I WAS DEEPLY IMPRESSED BY THE SUPPORT THE AFRICAN WORKERS GAVE.

NATIONAL DAY OF PROTEST
MONDAY, 26TH JUNE, 1950
Begins the all out struggle for Freedom.

Dr. J. S. Moroka, President-General of the African National Congress, supported by Leaders of the South African Indian Congress, and African People's Organisation calls upon all South Africans to REFRAIN FROM GOING TO WORK ON THIS DAY.

●

- DEFEAT THE SUPPRESSION OF COMMUNISM AND GROUP AREAS BILLS WHICH WILL TURN OUR COUNTRY INTO A POLICE STATE.
- DON'T ALLOW MALAN GOVERNMENT'S OPPRESSIVE FASCIST MEASURES TO CRUSH OUR LIVES AND LIBERTIES!
- FIGHT FOR FREEDOM – PASS LAWS AND POLICE RAIDS MUST GO! VOTES AND DECENT WAGES FOR ALL!

'Tis better to sacrifice all in the struggle for Freedom rather than live as slaves.

African, Coloured, Indian and European Democrats — FEEDOM NOT SERFDOM!

Nelson was also impressed by two Indians, Paul Joseph and Ahmed Kathrada. He admired their hard work and organizing abilities. Later that day, Nelson and Walter Sisulu went over and congratulated them.
In response to the May Day slaughter, the ANC called for a national stoppage on June 26. This time, Nelson and his friends were ready to co-operate with the Indian Congress, the communists and the trade unions.

Mandela was put in overall charge of the National Day of Protest. The stoppage was successful in the coastal towns of Durban and Port Elizabeth, and in Ladysmith. The co-operation of the Indians led the new ANC leadership to modify its isolationist position and led to...

1952 FORDSBURG

THE DEFIANCE CAMPAIGN

THAT'S MAHATMA GANDHI – WASN'T HE IN ASIA IN 1946, FIGHTING FOR INDIA'S INDEPENDENCE?

The Defiance Campaign against Unjust Laws was launched on June 26 – exactly two years after the Day of Protest. It coincided with the government's celebrations of 300 years of white presence in South Africa. Jointly organized by the South African Indian Congress and the ANC, the Defiance Campaign was largely inspired by the Indian Congress passive resistance campaign of 1946.

That's right, but he worked out his passive resistance tactics in South Africa. He spent 21 years in Natal from 1893. He lectured, wrote pamphlets, edited a newspaper and became the province's leading Indian spokesman. In 1907 he successfully used passive resistance to fight laws forcing Indians to carry passes. He returned to his native India in 1913.

WE CAN NOW SAY THE UNITY OF THE NON-EUROPEAN PEOPLE OF THIS COUNTRY IS A LIVING REALITY.

Nelson was appointed Volunteer-in-Chief of the campaign. This marked the end of his decade-long political apprenticeship and his graduation to the centre stage of political activism.

At the launch of the campaign, Dr Moroka and Walter Sisulu wrote a letter to prime minister Malan, demanding the same civil rights for blacks as those enjoyed by whites. Malan's secretary replied...

Office of the Prime Minister
Union Buildings
Pretoria

To whom this may concern:

It is self-contradictory to claim as an inherent right of the Bantu, who differ in many ways from the Europeans, that they should be regarded as not different especially when it is borne in mind that these differences are permanent and not man-made.

The government will under no circumstances entertain the idea of giving powers over Europeans to Bantu men and women.

Yours sincerely

(pp.D.F. Malan)

During the campaign 8,000 volunteers deliberately broke apartheid laws and were jailed.

HEY MALAN, OPEN THE JAIL DOORS! WE WANT TO ENTER, WE VOLUNTEERS.

Six laws were targeted as symbols of apartheid. Apart from the pass laws, which restricted the movement of blacks, the others had been passed by the Nationalist government between 1950 and 1952.

SO WHAT WERE THESE "UNJUST" LAWS?

THE GROUP AREAS ACT – divided up South Africa into areas designated for each race group. The aim was to bring racial mixing in all spheres of life to a minimum.

THE PARAMOUNTCY OF THE WHITE MAN MUST BE ENSURED IN THE INTERESTS OF THE DEVELOPMENT OF ALL RACES.

THANKS.

INTERIOR MINISTER

THE COLOURED VOTERS' ACT

Up to the 1950s, Coloureds were registered on the same voters roll as whites. The Act removed them and gave them their own ethnically elected representatives. Eventually they were completely disenfranchised.

THE BANTU AUTHORITIES ACT

Puppet authorities were set up for Africans in the reserves with government-appointed and salaried chiefs. It was the early stage of the bantustan policy which would divide blacks into tribal homelands and the beginnings of apartheid.

POPULATION REGISTRATION ACT

The Act was an attempt to preserve white privilege and exclusivity. Everybody was classified at birth as White, Native or Coloured. In this way people from other race groups could be prevented from trying to "pass off as white".

SUPPRESSION OF COMMUNISM ACT

The act was designed to suppress any form of opposition to the government that fundamentally challenged the doctrine of white supremacy. Communism was so broadly defined as to include any extra-parliamentary activity. Blacks, of course, were not represented in parliament and therefore had no legal means of presenting their case.

YOU DON'T HAVE TO BE A COMMUNIST TO BE BANNED UNDER THE ACT.

JOHN VORSTER
JUSTICE MINISTER

On July 30, 1952, 20 leaders of the Defiance Campaign were charged under the Suppression of Communism Act. They were found guilty but Justice Rumpff, dishing out nine-month suspended sentences said...

GUILTY ONLY OF STATUTORY COMMUNISM, WHICH HAS NOTHING TO DO WITH COMMUNISM AS IT IS COMMONLY KNOWN.

The Suppression of Communism Act was amended in 1954. It allowed the government to ban anyone for "furthering the aims of communism". The minister no longer had to give any reasons for the ban.

Dr Moroka was disgraced during the Defiance Campaign trial when he arranged for his own separate legal representation. He was ousted from the ANC presidency and his place was taken by Chief Albert Luthuli.

Nelson's rise in the ANC continued as a result, when he was voted president of the provincial branch of the ANC in the Transvaal.

GOING UP: LUTHULI, MANDELA, TAMBO & SISULU. **GOING DOWN:** MOROKA & XUMA.

ALBERT JOHN LUTHULI

Born to South African parents in Zimbabwe In the 1890s, Luthuli returned to his home in Natal as a child. He was educated at a mission school and became a teacher. In 1935 he inherited a minor Zulu chieftainship, but was frustrated by his political impotence. In 1946 he joined the ANC and became president of the Natal branch. He was a leading proponent of passive resistance. Because of his politics the government gave him an ultimatum: "Give up your chieftainship or the ANC leadership".
He refused to choose and the government stripped hiim of his chieftainship.

LUTHULI GOT INTO POLITICS BY ACCIDENT, WHEN HE WAS AT A MEETING TO ELECT A NEW LEADER FOR THE NATAL ANC. THE MEETING DISINTEGRATED INTO CONFUSION AND THE CHIEF JUMPED ONTO THE PLATFORM TO CALL FOR ORDER. HE WAS PROMPTLY ELECTED TO THE POSITION. THE FOLLOWING YEAR HE BECAME ANC NATIONAL PRESIDENT.

The Defiance Campaign rolled on through 1952. In October police provoked violence by firing on a prayer meeting in the Cape port of East London. A riot followed in which two whites died. This appeared to discredit the claim that the campaign was non-violent.

The government used this excuse to swoop on the homes of the ANC leadership.

Over a hundred ANC organizers were detained then banned. The campaign had to be abandoned.

The ANC realized the government wouldn't allow the Defiance Campaign to continue. The organization looked for new tactics. Nelson outlined the position in his presidential speech for the 1952 conference of the Transvaal ANC. But he was banned, which meant he was restricted to the Johannesburg area and was prohibited from attending the conference. The speech was read *in absentia.*

"LONG SPEECHES, THE SHAKING OF FISTS, THE BANGING OF TABLES, AND STRONGLY WORDED RESOLUTIONS OUT OF TOUCH WITH CONDITIONS DO NOT BRING ABOUT MASS ACTION. THE AUTHORITIES WILL NOT PERMIT A MEETING UNDER THE ANC. THESE DEVELOPMENTS REQUIRE THE EVOLUTION OF NEW FORMS OF STRUGGLE WHICH WILL MAKE IT POSSIBLE TO STRIVE FOR ACTION ON A HIGHER LEVEL THAN THE DEFIANCE CAMPAIGN."

The speech led in 1952 to the "M" Plan (Mandela Plan). In the face of mass bannings and detentions, and bans on public meetings, the ANC formulated a new strategy to be implemented by Mandela. The "M" Plan would see organizing move to a grass-roots level – block by block and street by street, with the ability to continue political activity despite the removal of leaders.

BANNINGS

BANNING orders were designed to restrict a person's movement and political activities.

A banned person was prohibited from attending any meeting. A meeting was defined as a gathering of three or more people – a banned person could only see one friend at a time. Banned people were not allowed to talk to other banned people.

There were other restrictions. A banned person was not allowed to enter certain buildings, including courts, educational institutions and newspaper offices. The homes of banned people were frequently visited by Security Branch (political police) and they were under constant surveillance. They were also required to report to the police at intervals. Banning orders were for two to five years and could be renewed repeatedly.

Although, in 1952, Nelson as a banned person could still be quoted, this was later changed. It became illegal to publish or quote a banned person.

Nelson was initially restricted under a series of banning orders for nine years. Even while he was in jail, he was banned. This was to silence him. For the 27 years he was behind bars it was an offence – punishable by a prison term – to quote or publish In his own country anything he had ever said.

The Nationalist government banned over 1,500 people during its period in power.

BANNED
NELSON MANDELA
ANC LEADER

BANNED
WINNIE MANDELA
ANC LEADER

BANNED
WALTER SISULU
ANC SECRETARY

BANNED
ALBERT LUTHULI
ANC LEADER

BANNED
STEVE BIKO
STUDENT LEADER

BANNED
YUSUF DADOO
INDIAN LEADER

BANNED
ROBERT SOBUKWE
PAC LEADER

BANNED
MOSES KOTANE
ANC LEADER

BANNED
FRANK MARQUARD
UNION LEADER

BANNED
DONALD WOODS
JOURNALIST

BANNED
BEYERS NAUDE
CHURCH LEADER

BANNED
CAN THEMBA
JOURNALIST

1952
FOX STREET, JO'BURG

MANDELA & TAMBO Attorneys

TO WHITE SOUTH AFRICA IT WAS BAD ENOUGH THAT TWO MEN WITH BLACK SKINS SHOULD PRACTISE AS LAWYERS...

...BUT IT WAS INDESCRIBABLY WORSE THAT THE LETTERS ON OUR WINDOW ALSO SPELLED OUT TO THE CITY OUR POLITICAL PARTNERSHIP.

SOUTH AFRICA HAS ONE OF THE HIGHEST PRISON POPULATIONS IN THE WORLD. JAILS A[RE] PACKED WITH AFRICANS IMPRISONED F[OR] PETTY INFRINGEMENTS THAT NO CIVILIZ[ED] SOCIETY WOULD PUNISH WITH IMPRISONMENT.

APARTHEID LAWS TURN INNUMERABLE INNOCENT PEOP[LE] INTO "CRIMINALS".

Nelson and Olive[r] Tambo set up the first black law practice in Jo'bur[g] in a shabby building across th[e] road from the magistrate's cour[t.] Chancellor House was one of the fe[w] buildings in whic[h] Africans were still allowed to hire offices. The building was owned by Indian[s] but in time the Group Areas Act would cast its shadow over this part of the city centre and landlords would [be] prosecuted if the[y] failed to evict the[ir] black tenants.

For years Nelson and Oliver worked side by side in their office near the courts. To reach their desks each morning they had to run a gauntlet of people overflowing from the waiting room into the corridors.

▼
68
▲

Tens of thousands of African residents of Sophiatown woke up one day in June 1953 to discover that they were living in just one such "wrong area".

1953 SOPHIATOWN

Close to "white" parts of Jo'burg it was one of the few urban areas where Africans could own freehold and where black and white mixed socially. Materially poor, it nevertheless harboured a rich black intellectual and cultural life. The government designated it "a black spot". It was targeted for demolition.

Advance

75,000 AFRICANS TO BE DUMPED ON BARE VELD

Inhuman Plan For Western Areas

MORE RAIDS ON CONGRESS OFFICES

Police Look for Treason

Get rid of ANGRY PAINS!

As soon as his banning order expired that June, Nelson – with Walter Sisulu, and Father Trevor Huddleston – addressed a large protest meeting at the Odin Cinema, Sophiatown. Police with sten guns broke it up.

THAT DAY I FELT THE FIERCE BREATH OF TOTALITARIANISM AND TYRANNY.

FATHER TREVOR HUDDLESTON

Fierce resistance continued through the 1950s. There were meetings, protests and marches, but eventually the government wiped Sophiatown from the map when two thousand armed police were sent in to enforce apartheid.

Residents were forcibly removed to the new township of Soweto (SOuth WEstern TOwnships). By November 1959, Sophiatown was dead.

In its place the government built a new white suburb called Triomf, which in Afrikaans means: "triumph".

SOPHIATOWN, THE CITY THAT WAS WITHIN A CITY, THE GAY PARIS OF JOHANNESBURG, THE NOTORIOUS CASBAH GANG DEN, THE SHEBEENIEST OF THEM ALL; SOPHIATOWN IS NOW BREATHING FOR THE LAST TIME...

'DRUM' JOURNALIST BENSON DYANTYI

JA, TRIOMF. WE CALLED IT THAT BECAUSE IT WAS A HELLAVAH TRIUMPH FOR APARTHEID.

Over three million South Africans were victims of forced removals during the 46-year rule of the Nationalists. Often they were dumped in barren land far from their homes and devoid of facilities.

In April, 150 delegates of all races met in Johannesburg to form the Federation of South African Women. The meeting was significant because it brought together women of all races.

The Federation led a series of protests against the extension of passes to women. These culminated in a massive protest in 1956 when 20,000 women marched on the Union Buildings in Pretoria – the seat of government power. They delivered bundles of protests and demanded to see the prime minister, J G Strijdom. They were told...

THE PRIME MINISTER IS OUT TODAY.

HELEN JOSEPH
CONGRESS OF DEMOCRATS

LILIAN NGOYI
ANC

SOPHIE WILLIAMS
AFRICAN PEOPLES' ORGANIZATION

RAHIMA MOOSA
(OBSCURED)
SA INDIAN CONGRESS

♫ STRIJDOM, YOU STRUCK A ROCK WHEN YOU MESSED WITH THE WOMEN. ♫

Many leaders who were banned were not allowed to attend. But in a message from his home in Natal, ANC president, Chief Luthuli asked: "Why will this assembly be significant and unique?" He answered his own question...

ABOVE ALL ITS MULTIRACIAL NATURE AND ITS NOBLE OBJECTIVES WILL MAKE IT UNIQUE, BECAUSE IT WILL BE THE FIRST TIME IN THE HISTORY OF OUR MULTIRACIAL NATION THAT ITS PEOPLE...

...WILL MEET AS EQUALS, IRRESPECTIVE OF RACE, COLOUR, AND CREED TO FORMULATE A FREEDOM CHARTER FOR ALL THE PEOPLE OF THE COUNTRY.

WHAT **IS** THIS FREEDOM CHARTER?

The Freedom Charter, which was adopted by the Congress of the People, has since been the principal document defining ANC policy.

SOUNDS LIKE SOCIALISM TO ME.

THE FREEDOM CHARTER

- The people shall govern
- All national groups shall have equal rights
- The people shall share the nation's wealth
- The land shall be shared by those who work it
- All shall be equal before the law
- All shall enjoy equal human rights
- There shall be work and security for all
- The doors of learning and culture shall be opened
- There shall be houses, security and comfort
- There shall be peace and friendship

Despite being banned and therefore prohibited from being present, Nelson attended the Congress of the People anyway – in disguise.

THE CHARTER IS BY NO MEANS A BLUEPRINT FOR SOCIALISM. IT VISUALIZES THE TRANSFER OF POWER NOT TO ANY SINGLE CLASS, BUT TO ALL THE PEOPLE OF THIS COUNTRY.

The Congress of the People represented the broadest democratic alliance in South Africa's history. Nelson realized that the government faced a single choice: crack down or crack up. He knew it was not about to capitulate.

He was right. It wasn't long before the government reacted.

After gathering its evidence the government sent in its police. In a well-orchestrated operation in December 1956 they swooped on the homes and offices of 156 leaders. They were arrested and charged.

These 156 Congress Alliance leaders were put on trial. The list was a "Who's Who" of opposition politics. It included Africans, Indians, Coloureds and Whites from every province and organization.

TREASON TRIAL

DECEMBER 1956

THE TRIAL WAS A GREAT PLACE TO MEET PEOPLE WE'D ONLY HEARD ABOUT BEFORE.

The Freedom Charter formed the basis of the treason charge. It was described as a blueprint for violent communist revolution. The trial dragged on for over four years. Although all the defendants were eventually acquitted, the trial disrupted the ANC.

Splits began to appear in the ANC and in Nelson's marriage.

In 1956 Nelson and Evelyn separated. What upset him most was the effect the breakup had on his two sons Thembi (9) and Makgatho (6), and his daughter, Makaziwe (3). Meanwhile the Treason Trial rolled on. During one lunchtime recess, Nelson's cousin Kaiser Matanzima arranged for him to meet a young social worker. Her name was Winnie Madzikela. After Nelson's divorce came through in 1957, they were married.

Of a marriage that was to last four decades, Nelson and Winnie spent only three years together. Three years after the wedding Nelson was sentenced to prison for life..

As another year of the Treason Trial was ending, new tensions tore at the ANC. Africanists in the Congress criticized the Freedom Charter because it promoted co-operation with whites. At the November 1958 conference of the Transvaal branch of the ANC in Johannesburg, a group of Africanists tried to repeat the Youth League coup of a decade earlier.

WE WANT NO CO-OPERATION WITH WHITES AT THIS STAGE.

PETER MOTSELE

AFRICA FOR THE AFRICANS! EUROPE FOR THE EUROPEANS; AND ASIA FOR THE ASIANS.

JOSIAS MADZUNYA

THE COMMUNISTS WANT TO OVERWHELM US.

After failing to gain control of the Transvaal ANC the Africanists, led by Robert Sobukwe, walked out of the conference and formed the Pan Africanist Congress.

PETER MOLOTSI

ROBERT MANGALISO SOBUKWE

Born in Graaff-Reinet in the Eastern Cape in 1924. Like Mandela and Tambo he was educated at Fort Hare and later became a lecturer at Witwatersrand University. His views were less extreme than those of some of his followers. He maintained that eventually whites could become genuine Africans. He was jailed for three years in 1960 and was then summarily transferred to Robben Island. He was released in 1969 and confined to Kimberley under a banning order, where he died in 1978.

1959
DURBAN

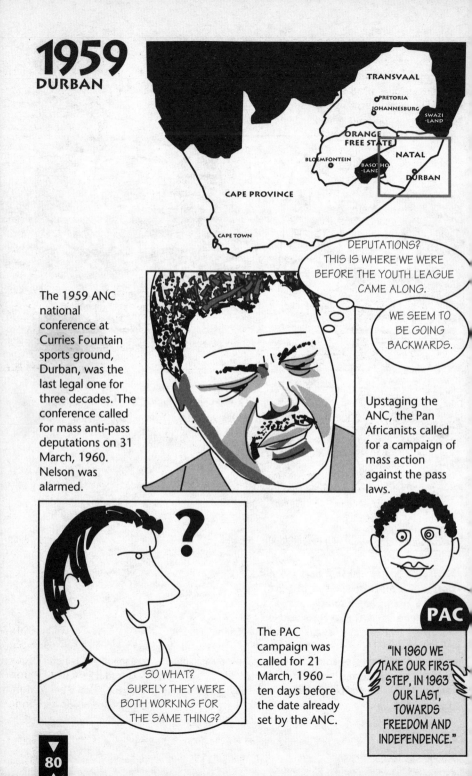

TRANSVAAL

PRETORIA
JOHANNESBURG
SWAZI-LAND

ORANGE FREE STATE
BLOEMFONTEIN
BASOTHO-LAND
NATAL

CAPE PROVINCE
DURBAN

CAPE TOWN

The 1959 ANC national conference at Curries Fountain sports ground, Durban, was the last legal one for three decades. The conference called for mass anti-pass deputations on 31 March, 1960. Nelson was alarmed.

DEPUTATIONS? THIS IS WHERE WE WERE BEFORE THE YOUTH LEAGUE CAME ALONG.

WE SEEM TO BE GOING BACKWARDS.

Upstaging the ANC, the Pan Africanists called for a campaign of mass action against the pass laws.

SO WHAT? SURELY THEY WERE BOTH WORKING FOR THE SAME THING?

The PAC campaign was called for 21 March, 1960 – ten days before the date already set by the ANC.

PAC

"IN 1960 WE TAKE OUR FIRST STEP, IN 1963 OUR LAST, TOWARDS FREEDOM AND INDEPENDENCE."

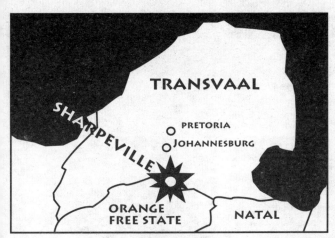

1960
SHARPEVILLE

On the morning of 21 March, Mangaliso Sobukwe and thousands of PAC supporters left home to present themselves without passes to police stations.

Sobukwe gave his supporters strict instructions to keep the demonstrations peaceful and not to be provoked into violence by anyone. Across the Transvaal and in the Western Cape there were several demonstrations, which in due course dispersed. At Sharpeville police station, however, the crowd refused to leave despite being buzzed by low-flying Sabre jets. A scuffle broke out and a policeman was pushed over. His colleagues panicked and opened fire, killing 69 and injuring nearly 200. Most were shot in the back, while fleeing.

PROTESTS demos and strikes swept the country. Anticipating a crackdown, the ANC sent Oliver Tambo out of the country. He crossed the border illegally and was helped by the Indian government to go to Britain.

27 MARCH

IN RESPONSE to an ANC call, there was an almost total stayaway of Africans from work. That evening, Nelson Mandela and Chief Luthuli publicly burned their passes. Thousands followed suit.

28 MARCH

OLIVER Tambo's flight proved timely. The government declared a State of Emergency. Nelson was detained in a massive roundup, along with 22,000 others.

30 MARCH

THE UNITED Nations Security Council called for the government to abandon apartheid and to take measures to promote racial harmony. Its Resolution 134 was adopted with two abstentions.

1 APRIL

8 APRIL

The Unlawful Organizations Act was passed. The ANC and PAC were...

BANNED

83

WHITE PANIC

THE RAND IS SLIDING AND SHARES HAVE SLUMPED.
THE PRIME MINISTER MUST TALK TO THE BLACKS AND ABANDON HIS POLICIES OR WE'LL ALL BE MURDERED.
ACTUALLY IT WAS THE PRIME MINISTER, DR VERWOERD WHO WAS NEARLY MURDERED LATER THAT MONTH...
...WHEN A CRAZED WHITE FARMER SHOT HIM TWICE IN THE HEAD.
MANY HOPED VERWOERD'S DEATH WOULD ALLOW THE GOVERNMENT TO PULL BACK FROM HIS EXTREME RACIAL POLICIES. SOME IN HIS OWN PART Y EVEN WANTED A NEW DEAL
BUT HE DIDN'T DIE. ERWOERD WAS SOON BACK AT HIS DESK...
...HIS FERVOUR RENEWED, HIS PRESTIGE ENHANCED...

Verwoerd's cherished dream was the White Republic. It went further than white supremacy, segregation or any other previous system in South Africa. It was an aggressive response to growing pressure inside South Africa and internationally for change. Verwoerd possessed two qualities that together were deadly: intellect and obsessiveness. Out of his fervour came the complex system of racial discrimination the world came to know as apartheid. Verwoerd did more than anyone else to draw up the practical blueprints on which it was subsequently built.

HENDRIK FRENSCH VERWOERD

Born in the Netherlands in 1901, Verwoerd came to South Africa with his family as a child. After being educated in Southern Africa, then Europe, he became head of Psychology at Stellenbosch University. In 1937 he founded and edited *Die Transvaler* newspaper. In 1950 he was appointed Minister of Bantu Affairs, till he became prime minster in 1958. Despite his origins outside South Africa, his politics were more Afrikaans than any Afrikaner's.

During the 1950s the winds of change began to sweep through Africa. Britain began the process of decolonization. In the United States, the civil rights movement had begun its own long march.
In 1959, the year after Verwoerd became prime minister, he unveiled his masterplan to counteract criticism.

GAMBIA (1965)

GHANA (1957)

SIERRA LEONE (1961)

NIGERIA (1960)

THESE BRITISH COLONIES BECAME INDEPENDENT IN THE 50s AND 60s

UGANDA (1962)

KENYA (1963)

TANZANIA (1960)

ZAMBIA (1964)

MALAWI (1964)

BOTSWANA (1966)

SWAZILAND (1968)

LESOTHO (1966)

WE CANNOT GOVERN WITHOUT TAKING INTO ACCOUNT THE TENDENCIES IN THE WORLD AND IN AFRICA.

Verwoerd's way of taking into account these international tendencies was a cunning scheme which turned a black majority into several ethnic minorities. This he presented as the granting of political rights to blacks. This scheme was...

THE BANTUSTAN POLICY

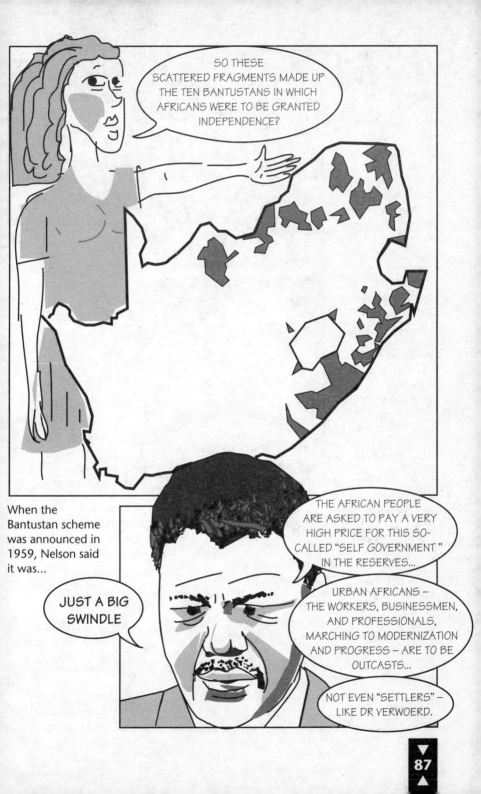

1961
LONDON

On 4 March, Dr Verwoerd arrived in Britain for the Commonwealth Prime Ministers' Conference. Freshly triumphant from a referendum that he claimed gave him a mandate to transform South Africa into a republic, he applied for the conference to readmit the country in its new incarnation.

HANDS UP FOR THE WHITE REPUBLIC

On 11 March, 1960, Dr Verwoerd told parliament that he wanted a referendum on South Africa becoming a republic. Ten days later came the Sharpeville massacre. Undeterred Verwoerd pressed on and whites voted on the proposal in October. Verwoerd achieved his cherished dream by a whisker when 52 per cent of the electorate voted for the White Republic.

The African and Asian prime ministers made it clear that the Republic of South Africa wasn't welcome.
On 15 March, Dr Verwoerd withdrew the application.

Playing the miracle worker once again, Dr Verwoerd turned defeat into victory when he returned to South Africa to riotous adulation from his white supporters. He told the country...

WHAT HAPPENED IN LONDON WAS NOT A DEFEAT BUT A VICTORY. WE HAVE FREED OURSELVES FROM THE AFRO-ASIAN STATES. MANY NATIONS HAVE TO GET THEIR FREEDOM BY ARMED STRUGGLE.

In Orlando, Nelson packed his bags and prepared to leave for Natal. He knew that the Afrikaner republic would close the door on even the mildest forms of black political opposition.

I WILL BE GOING AWAY FOR A LONG TIME.

MY FRIENDS WILL LOOK AFTER YOU. THEY'LL GIVE YOU NEWS OF ME FROM TIME TO TIME. LOOK AFTER THE CHILDREN.

1961

PIETERMARITZBURG

1,400 Africans from across the country converged on Pietermaritzburg on 25 and 26 March for the All-in African Conference to oppose South Africa becoming a whites-only republic on 31 May.

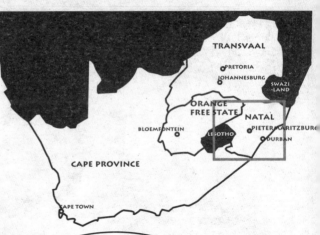

THE REFERENDUM WAS A FRAUD. WE DEMAND A NATIONAL CONVENTION NOT LATER THAN 31 MAY TO DETERMINE A NON-RACIAL DEMOCRATIC CONSTITUTION.

For the first time in nine years, Nelson wasn't under a banning order. He burst into public and made a huge impact. The All-in African Conference formed the National Action Council to campaign for a national convention. Nelson was elected its leader.

IF THE GOVERNMENT IGNORES US WE WILL STAGE COUNTRYWIDE DEMOS ON THE EVE OF THE REPUBLIC.

GO HOME NOW AND FORM LOCAL ACTION COMMITTEES.

MEANWHILE...
(BACK AT THE TREASON TRIAL)

Nelson left the conference and reported back to Chief Luthuli, who was restricted to the tiny district of Lower Tugela, near Durban. On 29 March, Nelson returned to Jo'burg to hear the verdict of the Treason Trial, now in its fourth and final year. By this stage all but 27 of the original 186 accused had been discharged.

From the state's point of view, the trial had been an expensive fiasco. For many of the accused it had caused suffering and misery. It contributed to the collapse of Nelson and Oiver Tambo's law practice.

All the remaining accused were found not guilty. Outside the courthouse the accused and supporters celebrated. Nelson knew the government would not leave him free for long. He left the trial and went underground.

NKOSI SIKELE I AFRIKA...*

*Nkosi Sikelele i Afrika (God Bless Africa): then the anthem of the ANC and now of South Africa.

Dr Verwoerd ignored the call for a national convention. Instead he mobilized the army and appointed a new justice minister, John Vorster – the toughest streetfighter he could find.

I TOLD HIM THAT YOU COULD NOT FIGHT COMMUNISM BY THE QUEENSBURY RULES.

HE AGREED AND SAID HE WOULD LEAVE ME FREE TO DO WHAT I HAD TO DO.

BALTHAZAR JOHN VORSTER

I TOLD DR VERWOERD TO LET ME DEAL WITH SUBVERSION AND REVOLUTION MY OWN WAY.

Not satisfied with bannings, house arrest and other draconian powers, Vorster, a trained lawyer, eagerly set about passing a succession of security laws that circumvented normal legal procedures. It looked to Nelson as if peaceful protest had come to the end of the road.

THE TIME COMES IN THE LIFE OF ANY NATION WHEN THERE REMAIN ONLY TWO CHOICES: SUBMIT OR FIGHT. THAT TIME HAS NOW COME TO SOUTH AFRICA...

WE SHALL NOT SUBMIT...

THE LIBERATION ORGANIZATIONS HAVE CONSISTENTLY FOLLOWED A POLICY OF NON-VIOLENCE – BECAUSE WE PREFER PEACEFUL CHANGE TO CIVIL WAR. BUT OUR PATIENCE IS NOT ENDLESS.

THE GOVERNMENT HAS INTERPRETED OUR PEACEFULNESS AS WEAKNESS BUT GOVERNMENT FORCE WILL NO LONGER ONLY BE MET WITH NON-VIOLENCE. THE CHOICE IS NOT OURS...

....IT HAS BEEN MADE BY THE GOVERNMENT, WHICH HAS ANSWERED EVERY PEACEABLE DEMAND FOR RIGHTS AND FREEDOM WITH FORCE. UMKHONTO WE SIZWE WILL BE AT THE FRONT LINE OF OUR DEFENCE.

WE WILL SKIM OFF THE NON-WHITE LEADERSHIP AS IT RISES.

For 17 months Nelson operated underground. The two months following the All-in African Conference were devoted to organizing the May stayaway against the white republic. The Verwoerd government put out orders for his arrest.

Nelson was the best publicist the ANC ever had. He eluded the police, popping up unexpectedly. For the next two months he was constantly in the headlines. The press dubbed him The Black Pimpernel. The government worked hard to stop the stayaway. Disinformation claimed that it would be violent. The PAC also criticized the stayaway. They said the white republic was of no concern to the African public. They told people to boycott it. Although there was some support across the country, the protest failed to disrupt the Republic Day celebrations.

20 MAY 1961. CALL TO THE JO'BURG SUNDAY EXPRESS FROM UNDISCLOSED PHONE BOOTH.

SO FAR WE HAVE ANTICIPATED EVERY MOVE THE POLICE HAVE MADE. I HAVE SO MUCH WORK THAT I DON'T EVEN THINK ABOUT ARREST. WE EMPHATICALLY DENY REPORTS THAT VIOLENCE WILL TAKE PLACE.

Meanwhile, that December, in Sweden, Chief Luthuli received the Nobel Peace Prize.

THE CREDIT IS NOT MINE BUT THE ANC'S. I INHERITED POLICIES THAT GO BACK 50 YEARS WHICH I HAVE BEEN HAPPY TO CARRY OUT

A week later on 16 December Umkhonto We Sizwe struck, with bomb attacks in Johannesburg, Port Elizabeth and Durban.

Umkhonto We Sizwe (Spear of the Nation) was set up by a group of ANC and Communist Party leaders as an independent armed wing – guided by the policy of the banned ANC. Nelson was its commander-in-chief. Umkhonto (or MK as it was commonly known) aimed to commit acts of sabotage against economically and politically symbolic installations in the hope of bringing the government to the negotiating table. Nelson gave strict instructions that people were under no circumstances to be killed or injured.

Post offices (as on the page opposite), telephone booths, pass offices and electricity pylons were blown up. The first attack by MK came on 16 December. It was accompanied by the distribution of the organization's manifesto...

We have always sought to achieve liberation without bloodshed and civil clash. We hope even at this late hour that our first actions will awaken everyone to a realization of the disastrous situation to which the Nationalist policy is leading. The government has interpreted the peacefulness of the movement as weakness; the people's non-violent policies have been taken as a green light for government violence. We are striking out along a new road for the liberation of the people of this country.

Afrika Mayibuye!

1962

In 1962 Nelson left the country clandestinely, without a passport. He toured West and North Africa setting up bases and arranging assistance for MK. Meeting up with his old friend and partner, Oliver Tambo, in Ethiopia, he inspected the first batch of recruits. He also went to Algeria, where he underwent training in demolition, weaponry, mortar-firing, military theory and tactics.

I WANT TO BE READY IF NECESSARY TO STAND AND FIGHT WITH MY PEOPLE

FOR THE FIRST TIME IN MY LIFE I'M A FREE MAN

ADDIS ABABA

ALGIERS

In Britain he met Labour and Liberal Party leaders... and he went sightseeing.

IT WASN'T ALL JUST WORK, WORK, WORK , YOU KNOW.

LONDON

In June, Nelson crossed back into South Africa at an unchecked border point. He was taken to Lilliesleaf Farm in a white suburb on the outskirts of Johannesburg, where his comrades, including Walter Sisulu, had set up an underground base.

In August, he travelled down to Natal to consult with Chief Luthuli. The Chief rebuked Nelson.

WHY DIDN'T YOU TELL ME THAT YOU WERE ABANDONING NON-VIOLENCE?

WE DELIBERATELY KEPT MK SEPARATE FROM THE ANC – WE WANTED TO PROTECT YOU FROM SUCH A DRASTIC CHANGE OF POLICY.

They departed – for the last time – on good terms. But the Chief never abandoned his lifelong commitment to non-violence.

POLITICS, POLITICS – THAT'S ALL YOU TWO EVER TALK ABOUT.

On 5 August, Nelson and a white friend set off from Durban to return to Lilliesleaf Farm in Jo'burg. Nelson was posing as the man's chauffeur.

JUST OUTSIDE HOWICK...

CECIL, I THINK THAT COP CAR'S TAILING US.

DAMN, NOW THERE ARE THREE OF THEM!

TO JO'BURG
TRANSVAAL
ORANGE FREE STATE
LESOTHO
NATAL
HOWICK
PIETERMARITZBU
DURBAN
INDIAN OCEAN

Nelson stopped the car...

He was taken to Marshall Square police station, in Jo'burg, and locked up in a cell.

YES, WHO'S THAT?

IT'S ME – IT'S NELSON... SO THEY GOT YOU TOO?

On 22 October, Nelson appeared in court charged with incitement to strike (for his part in the May Day stayaway) and with leaving the country without a valid passport. He showed his rejection of the legitimacy of the apartheid court to try him by wearing traditional dress and conducted his own defence.

AMANDLA NGAWETHU!*

THIS CASE IS A TRIAL OF THE ASPIRATIONS OF THE AFRICAN PEOPLE, AND BECAUSE OF THAT I THOUGHT IT PROPER TO CONDUCT MY OWN DEFENCE.

For four days Nelson carried on his defence, challenging the court and the white supremacy it represented. He attacked the prime minister, Dr Verwoerd, for having failed to respond to his letter calling for a national convention. And he defended his own conduct.

*POWER TO THE PEOPLE.

102

The prosecution rested its case on the fact that it was illegal for African mineworkers, employees of essential services and servants to strike. At the conclusion of the case the magistrate addressed Nelson...

HAVE YOU ANYTHING TO SAY?

YOUR WORSHIP, I SUBMIT THAT I'M GUILTY OF NO CRIME.

IS THAT **ALL** YOU HAVE TO SAY?

YOUR WORSHIP, WITH RESPECT, IF I HAD SOMETHING MORE TO SAY, I WOULD HAVE SAID IT.

On 6 November, the United Nations General Assembly voted for the first time in favour of sanctions against South Africa. The next day Nelson was found guilty on both counts and sentenced to five years' hard labour.

I HAVE NO DOUBT THAT POSTERITY WILL PRONOUNCE THAT I WAS INNOCENT AND THAT THE CRIMINALS ARE THE MEMBERS OF THE VERWOERD GOVERNMENT.

He was taken to Pretoria Central prison. Leaving the court, Winnie told the press...

THE GREATEST HONOUR A PEOPLE CAN PAY TO A MAN BEHIND BARS IS TO KEEP THE FREEDOM FLAME BURNING, TO CONTINUE THE FIGHT. MY HUSBAND SAID SUFFERING IN JAIL IS NOTHING COMPARED TO SUFFERING OUTSIDE JAIL.

Not long after, Nelson was transferred to the notorious Robben Island prison, just off the Cape Town coast. This became his home for over two decades. Walter Sisulu was sentenced to six years for furthering the aims of a banned organization – the ANC. Pending an appeal, he was granted bail – which he jumped on 20 April, 1963 and went underground. His voice was heard on Radio Freedom – the illegal broadcasting station of the ANC.

Two weeks later B J Vorster introduced his 90 Day Detention Law. Security Police were given the power to detain people incommunicado for up to 90 days. As Mr Vorster explained, this could be renewed indefinitely...

...UNTIL THE OTHER SIDE OF ETERNITY.

BALTHAZAR JOHN VORSTER
JUSTICE MINISTER

Torture and deaths in detention became routine.

SEPTEMBER 1963

"Looksmart" Solwandle Ngudle becomes the first political prisoner to die in detention

HE WAS TRYING TO HANG HIMSELF WITH SOME DENTAL FLOSS. ONE OF OUR MEN TRIED TO STOP HIM. THERE WAS A TUSSLE AND THE PRISONER FELL, SLIPPED ON SOME SOAP, TUMBLED DOWN 17 FLIGHTS OF STAIRS AND WENT FLYING OUT THE WINDOW OF THE 12TH FLOOR. HE WAS THEN HIT BY A PASSING POLICE VAN. THERE WAS ABSOLUTELY NOTHING WE COULD DO.

On 12 July, 1963, police rounded up 10 top ANC members at Rivonia. All were detained under the 90 Day Detention Law. Two, Andrew Mlangeni and Elias Motsoaledi, were tortured while in police custody.

Nelson was brought back to the mainland and then taken to Pretoria. Eventually the 11 were brought to court.

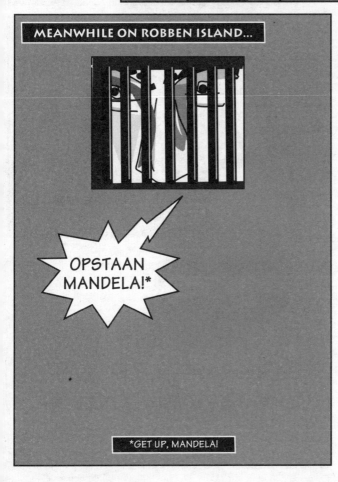

1963 RIVONIA TRIAL

On 9 October, Nelson found himself once again in court in Pretoria. Together with the other accused he was correctly identified as being a member of the MK high command.

THE ANC EMBARKED ON A POLICY OF VIOLENCE AND DESTRUCTION – A POLICY OF SABOTAGE – IN ORDER TO ACHIEVE THEIR ENDS.

PERCY YUTAR PROSECUTOR

ACTUALLY THE STATE'S CASE WAS A FIASCO... THE CHARGES WERE LUDICROUS, THE EVIDENCE WAS VAGUE AND THE CASE WAS UNSUBSTANTIATED.

NELSON WAS ALREADY ON ROBBEN ISLAND WHEN MOST OF THE ACTIONS HE WAS ACCUSED OF HAPPENED...

The prosecution case collapsed...

CASE DISMISSED!

thWACK!

but within seconds, while still in the court, the men were re-arrested.

The trial resumed on 3 December, with fresh charges of sabotage.

AHEM... LET'S TRY THIS AGAIN. YOU ARE ACCUSED OF RECRUITING PERSONS FOR SABOTAGE AND GUERILLA WARFARE FOR THE PURPOSE OF VIOLENT REVOLUTION...AND FURTHERING THE AIMS OF COMMUNISM.

They were also accused of conspiring to aid foreign armies to invade South Africa and of receiving funds from Algeria, Ethiopia, Liberia, Nigeria, Tunisia and "elsewhere". The charge sheet listed 193 acts of sabotage committed between 27 June 1962 and the date of the Rivonia raid.

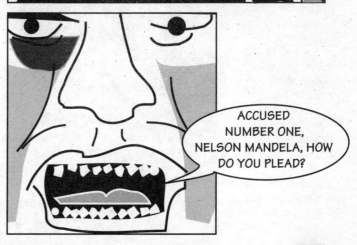

ACCUSED NUMBER ONE, NELSON MANDELA, HOW DO YOU PLEAD?

> THE GOVERNMENT SHOULD BE IN THE DOCK NOT ME. I PLEAD NOT GUILTY.

Nelson and the other accused agreed that they weren't interested in denying the charges.

DIE AFDELINGSRAAD VAN DIE KAAP
HIERDIE GEBIED IS SLEGS VIR BLANKES
OP LAS SEKRETARIS

THE DIVISIONAL COUNCIL OF THE CAPE
THIS AREA FOR WHITES ONLY
BY ORDER SECRETARY

" DO NOT DENY THAT I PLANNED SABOTAGE. I DID NOT PLAN IT IN A SPIRIT OF RECKLESSNESS, NOR BECAUSE I LOVE VIOLENCE. I PLANNED IT AS A RESULT OF A CALM AND SOBER ASSESSMENT OF THE POLITICAL SITUATION THAT HAD ARISEN AFTER MANY YEARS OF TYRANNY, EXPLOITATION AND OPPRESSION. **"**

They used the court to confront the apartheid state and to speak directly to the South African people and the world. From the witness stand, Nelson made his most comprehensive statement yet of his own ideals and those of the ANC.

"THE HARD FACTS WERE THAT 50 YEARS OF NON-VIOLENCE HAD BROUGHT THE AFRICAN PEOPLE NOTHING BUT MORE REPRESSIVE LEGISLATION AND FEWER AND FEWER RIGHTS. **"**

ANY KAFFIR TRESPASSING WILL BE SHOT

"I ADMIT THAT I HELPED FORM UMKHONTO. WE BELIEVED GOVERNMENT POLICY MADE VIOLENCE BY AFRICANS INEVITABLE AND THAT UNLESS RESPONSIBLE LEADERSHIP WAS GIVEN, THERE WOULD BE OUTBREAKS OF TERRORISM, WHICH WOULD PRODUCE RACIAL BITTERNESS. SECONDLY ALL LAWFUL MODES OF OPPOSITION HAD BEEN CLOSED BY LEGISLATION."

"WE CHOSE TO DEFY THE LAW. ONLY WHEN THE GOVERNMENT RESORTED TO FORCE TO CRUSH OPPOSITION, DID WE DECIDE TO ANSWER VIOLENCE WITH VIOLENCE. WHEN I WENT TO JAIL IN 1962 THE DOMINANT IDEA WAS THAT LOSS OF LIFE SHOULD BE AVOIDED. THIS WAS STILL SO WHEN THIS TRIAL BEGAN."

"THE IDEOLOGICAL CREED OF THE ANC IS, AND ALWAYS HAS BEEN, THE CREED OF AFRICAN NATIONALISM. IT IS NOT THE CONCEPT OF AFRICAN NATIONALISM EXPRESSED IN THE CRY, 'DRIVE THE WHITE MAN INTO THE SEA.'"

54 DEAD IN RIOTS
191 HURT
Army called out in Cape outburst

"THERE HAS OFTEN BEEN CLOSE CO-OPERATION BETWEEN THE ANC AND THE COMMUNIST PARTY. HISTORY IS FULL OF SUCH EXAMPLES. THE MOST STRIKING WAS THE CO-OPERATION BETWEEN BRITAIN, U.S. AND THE SOVIET UNION AGAINST HITLER. NOBODY WOULD SUGGEST THAT SUCH CO-OPERATION TURNED CHURCHILL AND ROOSEVELT INTO COMMUNISTS."

"Our fight is against real hardships – poverty and lack of human dignity. We do not need communists to teach us about such things... The complaint of Africans is not that they are poor and whites are rich, but that the laws made by whites are designed to preserve this.**"**

"Pass laws are among the most hated pieces of legislation. I do[.] whether a single African male not had a brush with the police his pass. Hundreds of thousand[s] Africans are thrown into jail e[ach] year under pass laws. Even wo[rse] is the breakdown of family life [it brings].**"**

"Children wander the streets because they have no schools to go to. This leads to moral breakdown and growing violence. Life in the townships is dangerous.**"**

"Africans want to be paid a living wage. Men want to have their wives and children to live with them. Above all we want equal political rights. I know this sound[s] revolutionary to whites in this country because the majority of voters will be Africans.**"**

There was international outrage at the sentence.

NEAR DURBAN

I APPEAL TO SOUTH AFRICA'S STRONGEST ALLIES BRITAIN AND AMERICA. IN THE NAME OF WHAT WE HAVE COME TO BELIEVE BRITAIN AND AMERICA STAND FOR, I APPEAL TO THEM TO TAKE DECISIVE ACTION FOR SANCTIONS THAT WOULD PRECIPITATE THE END OF THE HATEFUL SYSTEM OF APARTHEID.

CHIEF LUTHULI

LONDON

THE TIMES SAYS: "THE VERDICT OF HISTORY WILL BE THAT THE ULTIMATE GUILTY PARTY IS THE GOVERNMENT IN POWER – AND THAT ALREADY IS THE VERDICT OF WORLD OPINION."

THE UNITED NATIONS VOTED 106 TO ONE (THAT WAS SOUTH AFRICA) FOR THE UNCONDITIONAL RELEASE OF THE RIVONIA MEN AND ALL OTHER SOUTH AFRICAN POLITICAL PRISONERS.

NEW YORK

Despite all that, Britain, France and the US consistently used their vetoes to block mandatory sanctions against South Africa. It wasn't until 1977 that the West agreed to a mandatory arms embargo.

With the major leadership of the liberation movements behind bars, the Rivonia trial marked the beginning of the decade in which everything seemed to be going the government's way. Resistance was stifled, the state grew more powerful and for white South Africans, businessmen and foreign investors life seemed perfect. The panic caused by the Sharpeville massacre soon became a dim memory and confidence returned.

REPUBLIC OF SOUTH AFRICA   3c

DR VERWOERD
PRIME MINISTER

IT WAS WONDERFUL. SOUTH AFRICA WAS JUST LIKE ANY OTHER WHITE COUNTRY – EUROPE, AMERICA OR AUSTRALIA.. AND I GOT MY FACE ONTO A STAMP – MARVELLOUS!

FOR BLACKS POVERTY INCREASED. THIS WAS ENFORCED BY APARTHEID LEGISLATION.

CHILDREN GREW UP IN A WORLD WHERE VIOLENCE WAS NORMAL.

Robben Island is a windswept outcrop just off Cape Town. Conditions on the island were brutal. Winters are bitterly cold and wet. Prisoners were given only short trousers and no shoes. They slept on the floor on mats and had access only to cold water.

The Rivonia prisoners took the struggle against apartheid with them onto Robben Island. It began immediately. As they were being taken to the cells, the prison warders began trying to break down their morale.

MAAK GOU! SPEED UP! THIS IS ROBBEN ISLAND. WE WILL KILL AND BURY YOU AND NO-ONE WILL KNOW.

THAT MAY BE YOUR DUTY. OURS IS TO RESIST.

Nelson's conditions were the same as those of the other Rivonia trialists. They were all kept in solitary cells in a special isolation wing. Nelson lived in a grey concrete box 7ft square, lit by a 40 watt light bulb. He was confined for around 16 hours every day. When the prisoners were first admitted the authorities tried to create divisions between them. Nelson was offered a special diet which he turned down. On other occasions the warders systematically beat up the prisoners with pick axe handles.
Nelson was left alone.
Prisoners were at first allowed to receive and send one letter in six months. These were read by the prison censors. They were allowed two non-contact visits a year. Some conditions were improved over the years as a result of campaigns by the prisoners, in which Nelson took a leading role.

THE PRISON IS ABOVE ALL PUNITIVE. IT OPERATES TO BREAK THE SPIRIT, TO EXPLOIT WEAKNESS, UNDERMINE STRENGTH, DESTROY INITIATIVE AND PROCESS AN AMORPHOUS ROBOT-LIKE MASS. THE CHALLENGE IS HOW TO RESIST.

Wednesday
Week34

25

0500	Prisoners must wake up, use the toilet, slop out sanitary bucket, wash and shave.
0600	Prisoners must collect breakfast and fall in by 0630. NOTE: They must go by truck so they don't meet prisoners from other sections.
0700	They must clear seaweed or work in the quarry till lunch.
0800	
0900	
1000	
1100	
1200	Lunch is brought to prisoners in drums. They must sit on the ground to eat (even if it is wet after the rain)
1300	
1400	
1500	Prisoners must be taken back to prison by 1530 so warders can knock off.
1600	They must bath, eat their evening meal, and clear up pretty damn quick.
1700	They must be back in cells by 1630.
1800	
1900	
2000	They must be in bed by 2000 unless they have permission to study.
2100	
2200	
2300	Everyone must be in bed by 2300. Anyone caught reading must be charged.
NOTES	More or less the same as yesterday, and day before and in fact just about every other day.

NB: Whistling and singing are prohibited at all times.

In 1966 this picture of Nelson and Walter Sisulu in the Robben Island courtyard was smuggled out of the country. It was the last published photograph of Nelson till his release. Ironically for over two decades the world's most famous name was also its least known face.

In prison, Nelson continued his struggle – with his own emotions and with the authorities. His legal training taught him the advantage of hiding what he felt and relying on a cold, objective analysis of situations. As his anger against the system increased the more he learnt to temper it, forging the heat of his fury into a cold but highly effective instrument.

He kept a picture of Muhammed Ali in his prison cell and thought about strategy.

He began to look at politics from the government's point of view as well as that of the people. By understanding the regime's fears and perceptions he became better able to anticipate their moves and fight back more effectively.

FLOAT LIKE A BUTTERFLY...

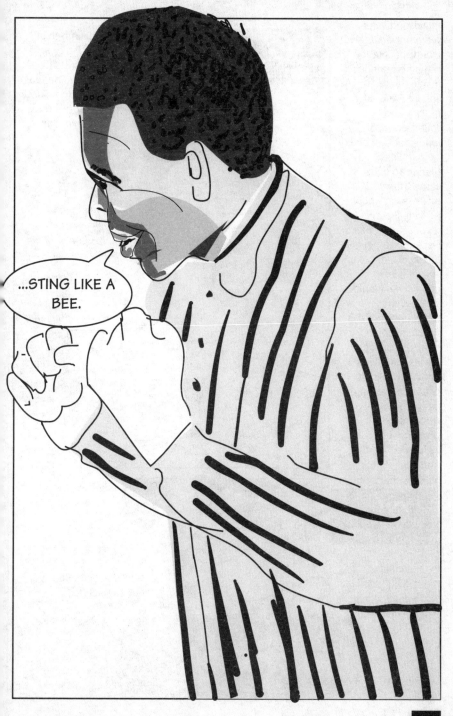

In prison there were tragedies and triumphs. Nelson remained confined inside those 7ft square walls as friends and members of his family died, while he remained unable to help, let alone attend funerals. In 1965 news leaked through that Bram Fischer had been arrested. Sometimes conditions would suddenly deteriorate, or the warders would treat the prisoners particularly harshly. The prisoners would know that something significant had happened on the outside.

1965 BRAM FISCHER ARRESTED

Fischer was a leading member of the banned Communist Party and had led the defence team at the Treason Trial. An Afrikaner, he was the son of a high court judge. After the Rivonia trial he abandoned his legal practice to go underground. He died in prison in 1977.

HIS SACRIFICE WAS GREATER THAN MY OWN. HE HAD TO ABANDON HIS TRIBE.

1966 DR VERWOERD ASSASSINATED

GET BACK TO YOUR CELLS YOU BLIKSEMS!* YOU'RE NOT GOING OUT TODAY!

*SWINES

When Winnie was persecuted by the authorities, there was little Nelson could do from prison. In 1967, he received his third visit from her in five years. The were allowed half an hour. They weren't allowed to make physical contact.

1967
CHIEF LUTHULI KILLED

One morning in July Chief Luthuli was found dead near the railway tracks. He had been knocked over by a train. There was some mystery surrounding the tragedy as the chief was familiar with the route, and had walked it on numerous occasions. The question surrounding his death was never satisfactorily answered.

1968
NELSON'S MOTHER DIES

DEPARTMENT OF PRISONS

APPLICATION FOR COMPASSIONATE TEMPORARY RELEASE

PRISONER'S NAME _Mandela, Nelson_

REASON FOR REQUEST _To attend mother's funeral_

PERMISSION REFUSED

After hearing, in 1969, that Thembi – his eldest son by his first marriage – had died in a car accident, Nelson returned to his cell and kept to himself. Only after Walter Sisulu noticed that he was being particularly quiet, and went and sat with him, did he confide the reason. One of his co-prisoners, Mac Maharaj, noted that Nelson never complained about his personal problems.

1973
VISIT BY JIMMY KRUGER

In December, the prisoners received their first visit from a cabinet minister – justice minister, Jimmy Kruger. They believed it was a kite-flying exercise to see if their release could be traded for compromises on their part. Kruger attacked them for advocating violence. Nelson gave him a lesson on the history of ANC's tactics – how they had only taken up armed struggle after exhausting all other avenues; and how they had made numerous peaceful approaches to previous governments.

I DIDN'T KNOW ABOUT THAT. WHY WASN'T I TOLD?

I THINK YOU'D BETTER GO BACK TO THE PRIME MINISTER'S FILES AND LOOK AT ALL THE LETTERS FROM THE ANC.

In the 1970s a younger generation of black consciousness leaders began arriving on Robben Island. After 1976 and the Soweto uprising there was a fresh intake. Although Bantu education had kept them ignorant of many of the activities of the ANC before its banning, all had heard of Nelson Mandela and were eager to meet him. He was always interested in hearing about the new developments in the country and was eager to listen to the views of the 70s generation. He asked them to present papers. They also found him a good social companion who enjoyed playing chess and dominoes.

The 70s generation was evidence of big changes taking place in South Africa. The economic muscle and confidence of Africans was growing. With it came a spirit of defiance the government would ultimately fail to quell.

1966
CAPE TOWN

Poplar Loans' Domes
CLARKES of MOWBRAY

The Cape Argus

NATIONAL RADIO

VERWOERD STABBED TO DEATH IN THE HOUSE OF ASSEMBLY

Dagger attack by messenger of Parliament

CERTIFIED DEAD AT HOSPITAL

THE PRIME MINISTER DR. H. F. Verwoerd died of with wounds inflicted on him in the House of Parliament this afternoon by a man wearing the uniform of a parliamentary messenger.

Man detained in stabbing works at Parliament

MRS. V.'s LAST KISS

Dr Verwoerd was replaced as prime minister by John Vorster. Vorster's power rested on his control of the police and the state security apparatus.

IF I CAN JUST GET THIS LID ON, THEN WE CAN GET ON WITH THE MEAL.

HENNIE
HEAD PEPPER CHEF

AMANDLA!

Vorster 's recipe for control was more eclectic. For the world at large he tried to present the face of reform. He travelled in Africa, met African leaders and even shook their hands. At home he gave South Africa's blacks a taste of something different. In 1969 he created the Bureau of State Security (BOSS) with his old Ossewa Brandwag comrade, Hendrik van den Bergh, at its head. Detention without trial, bannings, house arrests and deaths of detainees were routine.

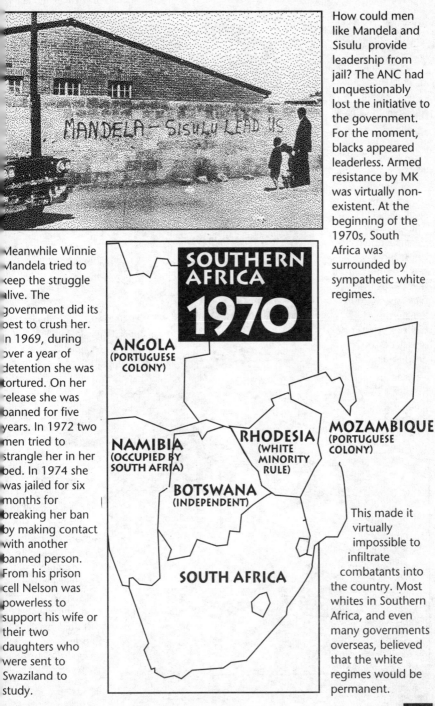

MANDELA - SISULU LEAD US

How could men like Mandela and Sisulu provide leadership from jail? The ANC had unquestionably lost the initiative to the government. For the moment, blacks appeared leaderless. Armed resistance by MK was virtually non-existent. At the beginning of the 1970s, South Africa was surrounded by sympathetic white regimes.

Meanwhile Winnie Mandela tried to keep the struggle alive. The government did its best to crush her. In 1969, during over a year of detention she was tortured. On her release she was banned for five years. In 1972 two men tried to strangle her in her bed. In 1974 she was jailed for six months for breaking her ban by making contact with another banned person. From his prison cell Nelson was powerless to support his wife or their two daughters who were sent to Swaziland to study.

SOUTHERN AFRICA 1970

ANGOLA (PORTUGUESE COLONY)

NAMIBIA (OCCUPIED BY SOUTH AFRICA)

RHODESIA (WHITE MINORITY RULE)

MOZAMBIQUE (PORTUGUESE COLONY)

BOTSWANA (INDEPENDENT)

SOUTH AFRICA

This made it virtually impossible to infiltrate combatants into the country. Most whites in Southern Africa, and even many governments overseas, believed that the white regimes would be permanent.

I GOT TO TRAVEL AROUND AFRICA, I GOT TO KICK A LOT OF ASS AND I GOT MY MUG ONTO A STAMP – LIFE WAS LEKKER*.

*SUPER

B J VORSTER

4c RSA

But then in the 1970s, it all started unravelling with a spate of strikes prompted by deteriorating black living conditions.

SMASH THE STRIKES, ARREST THE LEADERS AND PUT THEM AWAY INDEFINITELY.

Trade unions became one of the important movements during the 1970s that filled the vacuum left by the ANC. Neither Vorster nor his successors, despite all their efforts, proved able to stop the escalation of strikes.

THAT OLD WHITE MAGIC DOESN'T WORK ANY MORE, SIR. AS SOON AS WE PICK THEM OFF, THERE ARE MORE.

THEN TO CAP IT ALL, THE CARELESS PORTUGUESE WENT AND LOST THEIR COLONIES.

Angolan and Mozambican independence in 1975 shook white confidence in the region. Portuguese friendship and that of the white Rhodesians had helped South Africa to dominate the sub-continent. Rhodesia became independent in 1981.

1976
SOWETO

On 16 June, Soweto exploded when black youths rebelled against the imposition of Afrikaans as a medium of instruction in their schools.

EYEWITNESS ACCOUNT

THE POLICE ATTACKED, KILLED AND WOUNDED SCORES OF BLACK SCHOOLCHILDREN WHO WERE INVOLVED ONLY IN PEACEFUL PROTEST. AFTERWARDS A WAVE OF BITTERNESS SPREAD THROUGH SOWETO. IN FACT, WAR BROKE OUT...

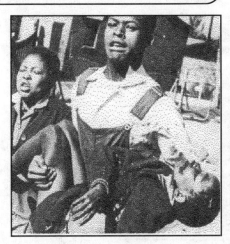

The protest became nationwide after police shot and killed 13 year-old Hector Peterson during a demonstration. By the following February, 575 people (nearly a quarter of them children) had been killed in the unrest that followed.

Even in the face of naked violence, protest spread to all sections of the black community. The Soweto Students Representatives Council successfully opposed rent hikes by the Urban Bantu Council – and finally brought about total collapse. The government was forced to rely increasingly on armed police to impose order. The student protests brought no educational improvements. In fact, for over a decade, tens of thousands of young blacks got virtually no formal education at all.

EVEN THE ANC CAME TO SEE THESE YOUTH AS THE "LOST GENERATION". THE BIG QUESTION FACING THE NEW GOVERNMENT IN THE 1990s IS....

CAN IT DELIVER TO THIS HUGE RADICALIZED, FRUSTRATED AND LARGELY UNEMPLOYABLE CONSTITUENCY?

Thousands illegally crossed the border to join MK training camps in a number of sympathetic African countries, including Zambia and Tanzania.

Winnie Mandela took a central role in the Black Parents Committee. The committee was formed both to help bereaved parents, but also to voice the grievances of Soweto residents. Winnie and other parents were detained without trial. She was released at Christmas 1976.

AND HERE'S YOUR CHRISTMAS PRESENT FROM MR VORSTER.

ANOTHER BANNING ORDER? BEEN THERE, DONE THAT.

As the anniversary of the Soweto uprising approached in 1977, the government exiled her to Brandfort – a small dusty village in the right-wing heartland of the Orange Free State. She was allocated a house without electricity or running water. She was banned and confined to the house at night, weekends and holidays under the guard of a policeman.

As the unrest rolled on into 1977, the Vorster government responded.

WE'LL PUT AN END TO THIS VIOLENCE.

DOES THAT MEAN YOU'LL CALL OFF YOUR POLICE?

NO WE'LL BAN THE BLACK ORGANIZATIONS AND DETAIN THE LEADERS.

In September 1977 one of these detained leaders died while in detention. His name was Steve Biko. He was the 46th political prisoner to meet his end at the hands of the security police.

STEPHEN BANTU BIKO

Born in 1946 in King William's Town in the Eastern Cape, Biko went to Natal University in 1966 to study medicine. He was first involved in the National Union of South African Students (NUSAS), but came to believe that as a white-dominated liberal organization it was incapable of representing blacks. He helped found the all-black South African Students Organisation in 1968 and became its first president. He was a leading figure in the Black Consciousness Movement of the 1970s. In 1973, Biko and SASO were banned. After that, he was constantly arrested and harassed by police. He was never charged with any crime, however. In August 1977, he was arrrested for the final time. He died from brain damage in detention.

Despite government attempts to stop them, by the end of the 1970s a whole range of grass roots organizations had arisen. The governmment failed to put the lid on this opposition, as it escalated through the 1980s. There were rent, bus and school boycotts, strikes and campaigns against removals. By the end of the decade, business was complaining that apartheid wasn't working. Even the government began to see this. The growth of the black population was outsripping that of whites. From a peak of 21% of the population in 1910, whites now made up only 16%. This was set to fall to 10% by the end of the century. The sums just didn't add up. There was a shortage of skilled labour and the unrest was bad for investment.

1978

...SEND IN THE ARMY!!!!

In September, John Vorster was given the push by defence minister P W Botha. This followed the exposure of a scandal involving the misuse of government funds. Vorster took BOSS chief van den Bergh down with him.

Botha was a party apparatchik who had built up his power base in the army. He had systematically built the South African Defence Force into the most awesome military machine on the continent.
He realized that for old-style apartheid, the game was up.

Botha adopted a complex strategy of reform and the increased use of force. He believed there was a total onslaught against South Africa from both outside and within the country. He tried to reassure whites by offering...

THE TOTAL STRATEGY

P W BOTHA IN HIS OWN WORDS...

THIS GOVERNMENT IS NOT SCARED OF SHOOTING. BUT WE SHOOT CIRCUMSPECTLY, SO WE CAN SHOOT AGAIN TOMORROW.

I'M GIVING YOU A FINAL WARNING: ONE MAN ONE VOTE IN THIS COUNTRY IS OUT. THAT IS – NEVER!

WE MUST ADAPT OR WE WILL DIE.

For blacks, he offered reforms, which included the legalization of trade unions. The government hoped that by doing this, and forcing them to register, it would be able to control them. The scheme backfired and the unions became increasingly powerful. Through the 1980s, pass laws were relaxed and replaced in 1986 with a policy of "orderly urbanization". Botha's hopes that limits on housing and work would stem the flow of Africans to the cities proved unfounded.

The president hoped that, by tinkering with apartheid and creating a black middle class, he could get the world off his back. But unrest continued and he responded with an increasing use of force. Detentions and executions of political activists increased (in contravention of the Geneva Convention). Heavy sentences were handed down in political trials.

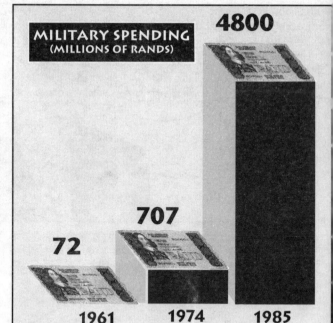

MILITARY SPENDING
(MILLIONS OF RANDS)

72 1961

707 1974

4800 1985

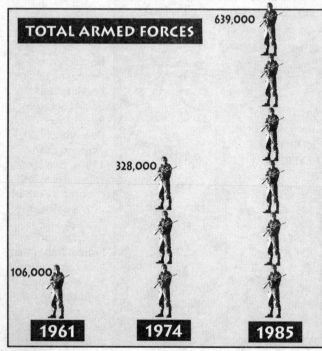

TOTAL ARMED FORCES

639,000

328,000

106,000

1961   **1974**   **1985**

But at the very heart of his Total Strategy was the deployment of the army to maintain "law and order". After 1984, troops were sent in increasing numbers into black areas to stop unrest.

Outside the country, the army tried to enforce compliance on neighbouring countries through the naked use of force. By 1983 every one of South Africa's neighbours had tasted this style of diplomacy. Destabilization tactics included: military strikes and bombings aimed at killing opponents of the SA government, as well as refugees; bomb attacks; financing of military opposition (Angola and Mozambique); War (notably against Angola).

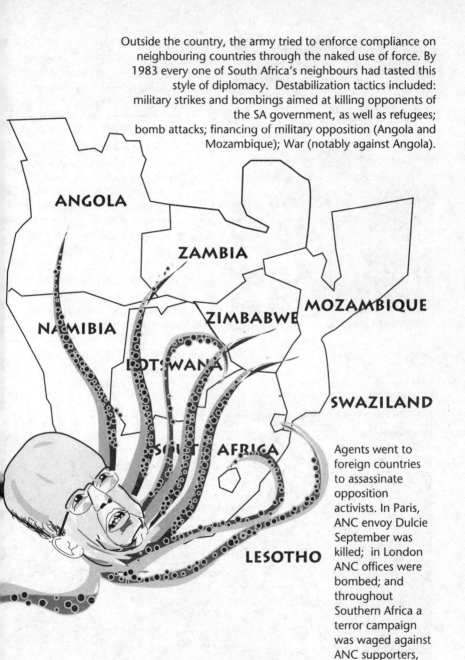

ANGOLA

ZAMBIA

MOZAMBIQUE

NAMIBIA

ZIMBABWE

BOTSWANA

SWAZILAND

SOUTH AFRICA

LESOTHO

Agents went to foreign countries to assassinate opposition activists. In Paris, ANC envoy Dulcie September was killed; in London ANC offices were bombed; and throughout Southern Africa a terror campaign was waged against ANC supporters, including Ruth First who was blown up in Mozambique.

1980

SUNDAY POST

MARCH 14, 1980

FREE MANDELA CAMPAIGN

Nelson Mandela had been silenced for 18 years but, despite government hopes, he hadn't been forgotten. As protest escalated, his name appeared more frequently on graffiti, banners and in songs...

MANDELA SAYS FIGHT FOR FREEDOM,
FREEDOM IS IN YOUR HANDS,
MANDELA SAYS FREEDOM NOW,
NOW WE SAY AWAY WITH SLAVERY,
IN OUR LAND OF AFRICA.
ROLIHLAHLA MANDELA,
FREEDOM IS IN YOUR HANDS,
SHOW US THE WAY TO FREEDOM,
IN OUR LAND OF AFRICA.

VULA BOTHA SIYANQONQOZA,
KHULUL' UMANDELA ASIKHOKELE
OPEN BOTHA, WE ARE KNOCKING,
RELEASE MANDELA, SO HE CAN LEAD US.

IN ALL MY TROUBLE AND SUFFERING,
MANDELA IS WITH ME,
EVEN AMIDST HIPPOS*
MANDELA IS STILL WITH ME.

*ARMOURED CAR

In June 1980, MK surprised the government by sabotaging a strategic oil refinery at Sasolburg. The refinery was heavily guarded. As the decade progressed, there were increasing sabotage attacks. During 1981 there were over 90 armed actions by MK against police stations, railway lines, power plants, military bases and recruiting offices. Often guerilla attacks were co-ordinated with protests. MK blew up buildings at a British Leyland factory when workers staged a strike there.

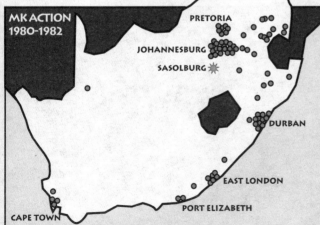

MK ACTION
1980-1982

PRETORIA
JOHANNESBURG
SASOLBURG
DURBAN
EAST LONDON
PORT ELIZABETH
CAPE TOWN

In Durban, when the authorities threatened to cut off power supplies to residents who refused to pay rent, MK sabotaged power stations supplying electricity to white homes and businesses in the area.

1982

As opposition grew the police minister complained....

THE ANC IS EVERYWHERE

THE GOVERNMENT SUDDENLY LEARNED ABOUT NEWTONIAN PHYSICS...

...DISOCVERING THAT EVERY ACTION HAS AN **OPPOSITE** REACTION.

P W Botha began thinking about reforms and moved Nelson and other Rivonia trialists from Robben Island to Pollsmoor prison in Cape Town. But Botha couldn't loosen his grip on the trigger. The army was still at large in the townships and over the borders...

1983
MITCHELL'S PLAIN

THE NEW CONSTITUTION WILL MAKE APARTHEID LESS BLATANT. IT WILL BE STREAMLINED AND MODERNIZED...

On 20 August 15,000 delegates converged on Cape Town to form the United Democratic Front. It was the broadest anti-apartheid gathering since the Congress of the People in 1955. The leaders included ANC veterans Archie Gumede, Albertina Sisulu and Oscar Mpetha.

REV ALLAN BOESAK
UDF OPENING MEETING

NONETHELESS, IT WILL STILL BE THERE!

The Front was a multiracial umbrella for 575 organizations. It endorsed the Freedom Charter and became a proxy inside the country for the ANC. Two years of boycotts, stayaways, strikes and protests followed.

But there were sinister stirrings from other quarters. In December, Gatsha Buthelezi, chief minister of the bantustan of KwaZulu, told a rally of Zulu migrant workers in Soweto...

THE UDF SEEMS TO BE ANOTHER FORCE FOR DISUNITY. THE NATIONAL PARTY, THE ANC AND THE PAC CANNOT SUCCEED WITHOUT INKATHA. FROM NOW ON INKATHA WILL ADOPT THE ATTITUDE OF AN EYE FOR AN EYE.

As leader of KwaZulu he rejected apartheid by refusing to accept phoney independence for his people. On the other hand he furthered the government's cause by opposing sanctions (called for by the ANC). He also testified against a woman who had allegedly helped the ANC's armed wing. Using his Inkatha Party he built up a regional power base in KwaZulu. In the 1990s press reports suggested a link between Inkatha and police dirty tricks against the ANC.

IF SOME WOULD BEAT US WITH A STICK, WE TOO WOULD PICK UP A STICK AND BEAT THEM. CONTINUING TO LABEL ME AS A SELLOUT IS GOING TO HAVE UGLY REPERCUSSIONS.

1984
CAPITAL RADIO

GOVAN MBEKI AND WALTER S SISULU ARE SPENT FORCES BECAUSE OF THEIR AGE. BUT THAT MANDELA... HE IS STILL IN GOOD HEALTH AND STILL REGARDED AS A LEADER.

PRESIDENT BOTHA SAID NELSON FELT SECURE IN JAIL AND PREFERRED TO REMAIN THERE FOR FEAR OF BEING KILLED IF HE WAS RELEASED.

Between March and December 1984, Nelson was offered release five times on condition that he agreed to banishment to the Transkei bantustan. This cat-and-mouse game continued throughout the 1980s. The government deliberately fostered speculation that he would be released. In 1985, he was held in hospital longer than necessary to remove his prostate gland. Winnie was allowed an extension on her visiting time in hospital. On his return to Pollsmoor, he was held in the prison hospital – away from his fellow prisoners.

1985
NEW YORK

Crisis struck for P W Botha when the Chase Manhattan Bank refused to roll over its loan to South Africa. Over the next two years, 90 US firms closed down their South African operations.

South Africa's townships became ungovernable. Nightly, the world watched as troops and police beat up and shot unarmed blacks. The Commonwealth – despite former British prime minister Margaret Thatcher's support for the Nationalists – condemned the government. America and Australia severed air-links. The US Congress defied President Reagan and passed the comprehensive Anti-Apartheid Act which promoted disinvestment. An increasingly desperate president Botha responded.

147

1985

JABULANI STADIUM

MY FATHER SAYS...

ZINDZI MANDELA

At a UDF rally in Soweto, Nelson's daughter Zindzi read her father's reply. It was the first time, since his imprisonment, that the people had heard a statement directly from him.

" I AM SURPRISED AT THE CONDITIONS THE GOVERNMENT WANTS TO IMPOSE ON ME. I AM NOT A VIOLENT MAN...

IT WAS ONLY WHEN ALL OTHER FORMS OF RESISTANCE WERE NO LONGER OPEN TO US THAT WE TURNED TO ARMED STRUGGLE. LET BOTHA SHOW THAT HE IS DIFFERENT TO MALAN, STRIJDOM AND VERWOERD. LET HIM RENOUNCE VIOLENCE...

I CHERISH MY OWN FREEDOM DEARLY, BUT I CARE EVEN MORE FOR YOUR FREEDOM. TOO MANY HAVE DIED SINCE I WENT TO PRISON...

I AM NO LESS LIFE-LOVING THAN YOU ARE. BUT I CANNOT SELL MY BIRTHRIGHT NOR AM I PREPARED TO SELL THE BIRTHRIGHT OF THE PEOPLE TO BE FREE...

WHAT FREEDOM AM I BEING OFFERED WHILE THE ORGANIZATION OF THE PEOPLE REMAINS BANNED?

WHAT FREEDOM AM I BEING OFFERED WHEN I MAY BE ARRESTED ON A PASS OFFENCE?

WHAT FREEDOM AM I BEING OFFERED TO LIVE MY LIFE AS A FAMILY WITH MY DEAR WIFE WHO REMAINS IN BANISHMENT IN BRANDFORT?

WHAT FREEDOM AM I BEING OFFERED WHEN I NEED A STAMP IN MY PASS BOOK TO SEEK WORK?

WHAT FREEDOM AM I BEING OFFERED WHEN MY SOUTH AFRICAN CITIZENSHIP IS NOT RESPECTED?

ONLY FREE MEN CAN NEGOTIATE. PRISONERS CANNOT ENTER INTO CONTRACTS. **"**

1986

Nelson declined to release Botha from the prison of his own policies. On the one hand, black resistance wasn't abating. On the other, Botha faced a backlash from whites. The right-wing Conservative Party was eroding government majorities in by-elections. In the 1987 general election the government polled just 52 per cent. Further to the right, the Afrikaner Weerstand Beweging (Afrikaner Resistance) broke up National Party meetings and threatened civil war.

Botha declared a State of Emergency and unleashed a period of tyranny. He banned people and meetings. There were shootings by police. There were mass arrests, detentions, treason trials and torture. And beyond the open use of force, the government sent death squads to assassinate the UDF leadership. It also collaborated in attacking UDF supporters in Natal and the townships.

Alarmed at the spiral of violence that was destabilizing the country, and its economic decline, a group of 61 white South Africans – mostly Afrikaners – went to Senegal. There they met an ANC delegation headed by Thabo Mbeki. A joint statement expressed unequivocal support for a negotiated settlement.

1987
DAKAR

On 18 July 1988, Nelson celebrated his 70th birthday in prison. The world paid tribute. In Wembley Stadium, London, the world's biggest ever birthday party was held for the world's most famous prisoner. The celebratory concert was televised across the globe. Then, late one evening the following month, Nelson was rushed to Tygerberg hospital, suffering from tuberculosis. By October, he had improved. In December, the government announced that he would not be returning to Pollsmoor prison. Instead he was moved to a warder's cottage at Victor Vester prison in Paarl – 50km from Cape Town.

1988

By the end of the 1980s Botha's policies had reached a dead end. Even elements in the army were looking for changes. The undeclared war in Angola was bleeding the treasury dry; Angolan and Cuban forces gained major victories in 1987, threatening to undermine the myth of South African invincibility.

FIRST THE GOOD NEWS...

OUR ARMY IS THE MOST POWERFUL SOUTH OF THE SAHARA. THE ANC CAN'T DEFEAT US MILITARILY.

NOW THE BAD NEWS...

THE ANC STILL HAS THE HEARTS AND MINDS OF THE PEOPLE AND ITS SUPPORT IS GROWING...

WE CAN'T DEFEAT THEM MILITARILY AND IT'S COSTING US MORE AND MORE TO MAINTAIN ORDER IN THE TOWNSHIPS...

INVESTORS ARE PULLING OUT AND THE ECONOMY'S GOING DOWN THE PLUG HOLE....

WE'VE GOT A STATE OF EMERGENCY AND THOUSANDS IN DETENTION, YET WE STILL CAN'T MAINTAIN LAW AND ORDER IN THE TOWNSHIP.

1989

VICTOR VERSTER PRISON

At the beginning of 1989 Nelson wrote from his prison to President Botha, calling for negotiations.

I am disturbed by the spectre of a South Africa split into two hostile camps – blacks on one side, whites on the other – slaughtering one another; by acute tensions which are building up dangerously in every sphere of our lives, a situation which, in turn, foreshadows more violence in the days ahead...

HOW COME I WAS THE ONLY NATIONAL PARTY LEADER WHO DIDN'T GET A LETTER FROM THE ANC? EVEN A POSTCARD WOULD HAVE DONE.

THE LATE B J VORSTER

PLEASE MR MANDELA YOU HAVE TO HELP GET ME OUT OF THIS.

THERE, THERE. YOUR ORDEAL WILL SOON BE ALL OVER.

Botha found himself with little room to manoeuvre. He had brought South Africa to a state of unprecedented crisis. But he refused to change direction and his party colleagues moved while he was weakened by a stroke. They forced him to resign and replaced him with F W de Klerk.

De Klerk was drawn from the conservative wing of the National Party. And from the start he made it clear that he was opposed to majority rule. But, he inherited a huge pile of problems that he realised he would have to deal with.

THE ECONOMY WAS IN TROUBLE. THE COST OF MAINTAINING APARTHEID BY FORCE WAS PROHIBITIVE.

THE ILLEGAL INFLUX OF AFRICANS FROM THE COUNTRY TO THE CITIES HAD PROVED UNSTOPPABLE.

BLACKS HADN'T BEEN TAKEN IN BY BOTHA'S CONSTITUTIONAL REFORMS.

AND EVEN SOUTH AFRICA'S FRIENDS WERE LOSING PATIENCE...

External and internal pressure was building up and it wasn't going to subside. De Klerk made a strategic calculation...

...OUR PARTY HAS A FIVE DECADE TRACK RECORD OF SCHEMING AND GERRYMANDERING.

WE'LL OUTMANOUEVRE THEM.

SO LET'S RELEASE MANDELA

Nelson set the conditions for his own release.

END THE STATE OF EMERGENCY, UNBAN THE ANC, AND ALLOW FREE POLITICAL ACTIVITY.

De Klerk agreed. In February 1990, he announced the unbanning of the ANC, the Pan Africanist Congress, the Communist Party and 33 other organizations. While maintaining the five-year-old State of Emergency, for the first time a National Party leader spoke about negotiating on the basis of votes for all.

On Sunday, 11 February 1990, at around 4pm, the world watched as Nelson stepped out of prison after 27 years. He took Winnie's hand and together they gave the ANC salute.

UNFORTUNATELY, IT WASN'T QUITE THAT SIMPLE. APARTHEID WAS STILL IN PLACE...

...AND SO WAS THE GOVERNMENT THAT PUT IT THERE.

The ANC, for its part, faced a series of problems. It had to:

❏ bring its radicalized youth within the organization's discipline;

❏ reconcile internal divisions, including those between militants and moderates – those schooled in defiant resistance and pragmatists who accepted a need to compromise;

❏ transform an underground revolutionary organization into a mass-based political party operating in an entirely new climate of legality.

At a huge rally in Cape Town on the day of his release, Nelson spoke to his supporters for the first time in three decades.

I STAND BEFORE YOU, NOT AS A PROPHET, BUT AS A HUMBLE SERVANT.

THE FACTORS WHICH NECESSITATED ARMED STRUGGLE STILL EXIST. WE HOPE THAT A CLIMATE CONDUCIVE TO A NEGOTIATED SETTLEMENT WILL EXIST SOON...

In the four years after his release, Nelson's diary was full. In between negotiating a new constitution, giving interviews and heading the consolidation of the ANC, he embarked on a punishing schedule of meetings both inside South Africa and abroad.

JUNE 1990
US CONGRESS

THE DAY MAY NOT BE FAR, WHEN WE WILL BORROW THE WORDS OF THOMAS JEFFERSON AND SPEAK OF THE WILL OF THE SOUTH AFRICAN PEOPLE.

In March the ANC national executive named him ANC deputy president. Later that month he retraced his 1962 tour of Africa ending up in Sweden where he had an emotional reunion with his old friend and partner, Oliver Tambo, who was recovering from a stroke.

WHEN WE WANTED TO TAKE UP ARMS AND APPROACHED WESTERN GOVERNMENTS WE NEVER SAW ANY BUT THE MOST JUNIOR MINISTERS...

...IN CUBA WE WERE RECEIVED BY THE HIGHEST OFFICIALS AND OFFERED WHATEVER WE WANTED.

YOUR RIGHT TO DETERMINE YOUR OWN DESTINY WAS USED TO DENY US THE CHANCE TO DETERMINE OUR OWN.

THAT WAS A NICE SPEECH – BUT A BIT SHORT.

JULY 1991
CUBA

MAY 1993
HOUSE OF COMMONS

ONE OF THE MOST PAINFUL EXPERIENCES IS TO SEE YOUR WIFE BEING HOUNDED FROM JOB TO JOB, YOUR CHILDREN BEING PERSECUTED, POLICE BREAKING INTO YOUR HOUSE AT MIDNIGHT AND EVEN ASSAULTING YOUR WIFE, WHEN YOU ARE ABSOLUTELY HELPLESS IN JAIL.

In the midst of Nelson's growing international prestige, personal tragedy struck with the break-up of his marriage to Winnie who had become an increasingly controversial figure. During the 80s she voiced support for the practice of "necklacing" (putting a tyre round the neck of a victim and setting it alight). Later, her growing radicalism distanced her from the ANC leadership. Fighting back tears, Nelson told the media in May 1992 that they had decided to separate. The announcement came in the wake of a trial which found Winnie guilty of involvement in the kidnapping and death of a young Sowetan boy, Stompie Moeketsie Seipei, in 1989. She was sentenced to six years, but was given a supended sentence on appeal.

In May 1990, the newly unbanned ANC and the government signed an agreement to repeal repressive laws, release political prisoners and create an appropriate climate for negotiations. Nelson persuaded the ANC to suspend the armed struggle in August 1990.

APRIL 1990

MAJORITY RULE IS NOT SUITABLE FOR SOUTH AFRICA, BECAUSE IT WILL LEAD TO THE DOMINATION OF MINORITIES.

HANG MANDELA

BEVRY BAREND

OUR POLICY? BRAAIVLEIS, DOP EN OORLOG!*

*BARBECUE, BOOZE AND WAR

EUGENE TERRE BLANCHE

The following month, the government lifted the State of Emergency (except in Natal) – one of Nelson's preconditions for real talks. As events moved slowly towards full-blown constitutional negotiations, it became clear that De Klerk still clung to race-based notions. Eugene Terre Blanche, leader of the neo-nazi AWB, accused the government of capitulating and threatened open warfare. However, another kind of violence was a more serious threat to the process...

One of the biggest problems facing the ANC was ongoing violence. This was most marked in Natal, where Chief Buthelezi's conservative Inkatha movement had been under challenge since the mid-1980s. Between 1987 and 1990, over 3,000 people had died.

MANY BELIEVED THAT THIS WAS PART OF A STRATEGY BY THE SECURITY SERVICES TO WEAKEN THE ANC.

THE VIOLENCE WOULD DISCREDIT THE ANC, WHILE FOSTERING THE NOTION THAT BLACKS WERE WARRING SAVAGES UNABLE TO GOVERN.

FOUR YEARS LATER...

The Guardian

SA police behind Zulu arms

Inkatha's claim of sovereignty raises threat of civil war

THE GUARDIAN
LONDON, SATURDAY 19 MARCH, 1994

Mandela argued strongly that a sinister "Third Force" was fuelling conflict between Inkatha and ANC supporters. Exactly two weeks after his release in 1990, Nelson went to Natal to attempt to heal the rift. He praised Chief Buthelezi for his stand against apartheid and he told a meeting of ANC followers to throw their weapons into the sea. But the violence continued unabated, right up to the eve of elections in April 1994.

HMMMM...

AUGUST 1990

In August, as the ANC suspended its armed struggle, the Natal violence burst into the Johannesburg townships. Gunmen struck on the commuter trains that took blacks to and from work.

A peace accord, signed in January 1991, between Inkatha and the ANC failed to end the violence. Nelson wrote to President de Klerk in April, arguing that three things pointed to a co-ordinated campaign.

APRIL 1991

❑ Those responsible are distinguished by their capacity to evade detection by the police.

❑ On at least three occasions when the authorities have been called to avert violence, they have themselves committed acts of violence.

❑ These acts of violence coincide uncannily with ANC-launched campaigns.

162

As 1991 drew to a close, 18 organizations sat down together at the World Trade Centre in Johannesburg to launch the Convention for a Democratic South Africa (Codesa). Codesa's task was to negotiate a new constitution for South Africa. Participants included political parties and 10 bantustan administrations. The talks were boycotted by the white right wing. Two Africanist organizations, the PAC and Azanian People's Organization, also refused to take part.

De Klerk's hand was strengthened in May 1992, when a whites-only referendum delivered a two-thirds majority in favour of negotiations. But problems emerged when Chief Buthelezi threatened to boycott the second session of Codesa, because the Zulu king was refused status as a negotiator.

MAY 1992

NEGOTIATIONS ARE A SITE OF STRUGGLE. CONSEQUENTLY, THE CODESA NEGOTIATIONS MUST BE SUPPORTED BY OTHER FORMS OF STRUGGLE.

On 17 June, over 40 people were shot or hacked to death in a midnight attack on shacks at the Boipatong squatter camp near Johannesburg. Eyewitnesses reported seeing police trucks ferrying alleged Inkatha supporters to the scene. President de Klerk denounced the massacre and went to Boipatong where he was met by hostile residents. After he had left police opened fire on crowds, causing further deaths.

JUNE 1992

When Nelson went to Boipatong a crowd of youths sang...

♪ MANDELA YOU BEHAVE LIKE A LAMB WHILE WE ARE BEING SLAUGHTERED ♪

I CAN NO LONGER EXPLAIN TO OUR PEOPLE WHY WE KEEP ON TALKING PEACE TO MEN WHO ARE CONDUCTING WAR AGAINST US

SPEECH TO RESIDENTS OF BOIPATONG

The ANC broke off talks, demanding that de Klerk take action to stop the violence. For nine months there was a stalemate. The ANC, in alliance with the Communist Party and trade unions, launched a campaign of mass action to pressurize the government.

On 3-4 August the alliance called a general strike in support of negotiations. Four million workers took part in one of the largest stayaways in South African history. A hundred thousand marchers converged on the Union Buildings in Pretoria – the seat of government – where Nelson addressed them.

IT IS TIME FOR THE GOVERNMENT TO ABANDON ITS PATH. WHILE PURSUING NEGOTIATIONS, IT SEEKS TO WEAKEN THE DEMOCRATIC FORCES.

Early the next month the army of the Ciskei bantustan fired on a peaceful pro-ANC march killing 28 and wounding 200. The ANC blamed the South African government. The attack brought the transition process to the brink of disaster. This was narrowly avoided when the government agreed to take measures to reintegrate the nominally independent bantustans into the South African system. Both sides then agreed to a de Klerk-Mandela summit meeting to break the Codesa deadlock.

SEPTEMBER 1992

165

After a series of meetings which excluded other parties, the two leaders signed the Record of Understanding, which laid the groundwork for new negotiations. They agreed to:

❑ an elected constituent assembly to draft the new constitution;

❑ the installation of an interim government;

❑ the release of political prisoners;

❑ steps to end political violence.

SEPTEMBER 1992

RATTLE
RATTLE
RATTLE

Chief Buthelezi reacted sharply to the bilateral talks.

WE WEREN'T CONSULTED SO WE WON'T ABIDE BY THOSE DECISIONS.

However, when the government tried to initiate talks with Buthelezi's Inkatha Freedom Party, the Chief showed no interest. Instead he formed an alliance with assorted right-wing organizations and bantustan administrations to oppose ANC-National Party dominated talks. Not long afterwards the legislative assembly of his KwaZulu bantustan adopted a consitition that would make it an autonomous state in the new South Africa.

OCTOBER 1992

President de Klerk apologised (conditionally) for apartheid.

SORRY ABOUT APARTHEID EVERYBODY – WE DIDN'T REALLY MEAN IT.

In a major concession to white fears, the ANC proposed "sunset clauses", which would lead to a power-sharing government after elections. The idea was first mooted by the Communist Party and was sponsored by ANC militant Chris Hani. Hani's support for compromise was significant – because of his militant credentials he avoided accusations of betrayal.

At the end of the year the government dismissed 23 senior army officers for alleged involvement in destabilization activities.

NOVEMBER 1992

SUNSET CLAUSES

CHRIS HANI

A charismatic figure, Chris Hani enjoyed support among militants and moderates in the ANC and was revered by black youth. An opinion poll in November 1992 judged him the most popular leader in the country after Nelson Mandela. He joined the Communist Party and MK in 1962 and saw action in Rhodesia (Zimbabwe) where he fought alongside the ZIPRA liberation army. In 1987 he replaced Joe Slovo as MK chief-of-staff, a position he subsequently resigned to take over leadership of the Communist Party.

APRIL 1993

Negotiations with all the major parties (including Inkatha), taking part, resumed in the new year. In a tragic irony, Chris Hani, the man who helped get talks back on track was assassinated as he stepped out of his car at his home in Boksburg – a town near Johannesburg. The assassin, who was a member of the white right-wing was captured.

Hani's assassination touched deep fears among all South Africans. A descent into bloody civil war looked like a distinct possibility. For three consecutive nights the nation watched as Nelson appeared on prime-time television calling for calm. This marked a psychological turning point. While President de Klerk adopted a low profile the ANC president was able to hold the country together. Pushing the advantage he had gained, Nelson called for the immediate setting of an election date.

APRIL 1993

HAMBA KAHLE COMRADE HANI

1942-1993

*FAREWELL COMRADE HANI

WE WARN ALL WHO SEEK TO IMPOSE ENDLESS NEGOTIATIONS THAT ANY FURTHER DELAY WILL DISCREDIT THE PROCESS AND PLACE ON THE AGENDA CHANGE BY OTHER MEANS.

CHRIS HANI'S FUNERAL, 19 APRIL

Later that month the ANC lost another leader when Oliver Tambo died after a long illness.

THE COUNTDOWN TO DEMOCRACY HAS BEGUN

Barely a month later Codesa voted to set the date for elections: 27 April 1994. The right-wing Conservative Party and Buthelezi opposed the date and their delegations walked out of the negotiations.

SEPTEMBER

The Norwegian Nobel Committee announced that Nelson Mandela and F W de Klerk were to share the Nobel Peace Prize for their part in diamantling apartheid.

VOLKSTAAT

DECEMBER

In December, for the first time in its history South Africa had an interim multiracial administration when the Transitional Executive Council was installed. But violence continued to endanger the transition and Chief Buthelezi and the right-wing Freedom Alliance still threatened civil war unless KwaZulu was given autonomy and the Afrikaners a volkstaat (homeland). Bloodshed and mayhem in Natal continued and it looked like the entire election could be disrupted.

KwaZulu gears up for guerrilla war

'Stra delay Goni'

Shadey Nas

A kwaZulu commander is training the 'five rand brigade' in Vietnam-style tactics to defeat an ANC government, reports **Chris McGreal**

THE commander of the kwa-Zulu Self Protection Unit, former intelligence officer Philip Powell, openly admits the 5 000-strong brigade is being prepared for the day the Inkatha-controlled kwaZulu authority is stripped of its power — and resistance to an ANC-led government goes underground.

Although supposedly training for self-defence, the kwaZulu Police (KZP) is teaching the self-protection outfits to handle automatic weapons and ambush vehicles. The regional com...

The right wing continued to threaten open warfare and Chief Buthelezi warned that if Kwazulu wasn't given autonomy the Natal violence would escalate. In February, the negotiating parties returned to the World Trade Centre to make constitutional changes to accommodate Chief Buthelezi and Afrikaners demanding a volkstaat. The principle of self-determination was accepted but the concessions failed to draw Inkatha and the right-wing Afrikaner Volksfront (People's Front) into the elections.

MARCH 1994

at Mmabatho

ng place amid huthatswana e Mmabatho

Minutes after this photograph was taken, shocked white South Africans watched as these these neonazi paramilitaries were summarily executed by a black soldier in front of television cameras.

when a barricade was erected at the front of the hotel to prevent any infiltration by agitators, security force or the marauding hordes that plagued the Mega City shopping complex for th...

By Thursday, due to...

A popular uprising against the government of the Bophutatswana bantustan resonated around South Africa. The army and police mutinied. In an attempt to shore up his regime, the territory's President Mangope asked white right wingers to help. Hundreds of neonazis converged on the capital Mmabatho and South Africa watched as they were routed by the bantustan army. Television images of armed whites being ignominiously defeated by blacks sent a powerful message about their own invincibility to South African whites.

Pan African Congress of Azania — PAC

Sports Organisation for Collective Contributions and Equal Rights — SOCCER

The Keep It Straight and Simple Party — KISS

Vryheidsfront - Freedom Front — VF-FF

Women's Rights Peace Party — WRPP

Workers List Party — WLP

Ximoko Progressive Party — XPP

Africa Muslim Party — AMP

African Christian Democratic Party — ACDP

African Democratic Movement — ADM

African Moderates Congress Party — AMCP

African National Congress — ANC

Democratic Party / Demokratiese Party — DP

Dikwankwetla Party of South Africa — DPSA

Federal Party — FP

Luso - South African Party — LUSAP

Minority Front — MF

National Party - Nasionale Party — NP

INKATHA □

Bophutatswana was reincorporated into South Africa under the administration of the Transitional Executive Council. Two weeks later the Ciskei bantustan's military ruler resigned. At the last minute the Afrikaner Volksfront – an ally of Chief Buthelezi – announced that it would take part in the elections after all. These events left Buthelezi isolated but he still insisted on boycotting the elections. He demanded the restoration of the Zulu kingdom under his nephew King Goodwill. Buthelezi threatened to secede from South Africa. His supporters were whipped up and there was an upsurge in political violence. In April the TEC declared a state of emergency in Natal and sent in the army. One week before the election Buthelezi agreed to take part.

In a last abortive attempt to disrupt the transition, a group of rightwing terrorists launched a bombing campaign. A number of people died, but this failed to stop the elections. After Jan Smuts international airport was attacked, the police swooped on a farm in the Transvaal and cracked a terror gang. There were no further blasts. Despite organizational hiccups the elections were carried out peacefully. Millions waited patiently for hours to vote for the first time.

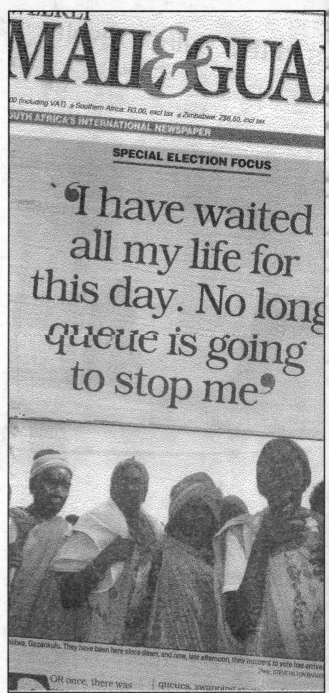

MAIL&GUA

30 (including VAT) ✳ Southern Africa: R3.00, excl tax ✳ Zimbabwe: Z$6.50, incl tax

SOUTH AFRICA'S INTERNATIONAL NEWSPAPER

SPECIAL ELECTION FOCUS

'I have waited all my life for this day. No long queue is going to stop me'

...twa, Gazankulu. They have been here since dawn, and now, late afternoon, their moment to vote has arrived
Pics: STEVE HILTON-BARBER

OR once, there was | queues, swarming...

There was never any doubt that the ANC would sweep to victory. On 2 May President de Klerk conceded defeat to Nelson Mandela.

TIMES

TUESDAY MAY 3 1994

Mandela 'free at last'

Shots and dance greet South Africa new day

THE CALM AND TOLERANT ATMOSPHERE DURING THE ELECTION DEPICTS THE SOUTH AFRICA WE CAN BE. WE MIGHT HAVE OUR DIFFERENCES BUT WE ARE ONE PEOPLE WITH A COMMON DESTINY...

WE MUST BEGIN TO BUILD A BETTER LIFE FOR ALL SOUTH AFRICANS. THIS MEANS CREATING JOBS, BUILDING HOUSES, PROVIDING EDUCATION AND BRINGING PEACE AND SECURITY FOR ALL.

Nelson Mandela inherited from the National Party a country of roughly 50 million people. Of these, six million were unemployed, nine million were destitute, 10 million had no access to running water and 23 million had no electricity. Among adult blacks 60% were illiterate and fewer than 50 % of black children under 14 went to school. The gap in living standards between black and white still remained. Infant mortality among Africans ran at 80 deaths per 1,000 but just seven among whites. The struggle had just begun...

NKOSI SIKELEL' I-AFRIKA

South Africa's new National Anthem

NKOSI SIKELEL' I-AFRIKA
MALUPHAKANYISW'UDOMO LWAYO
YIZWA IMITHANDAZO YETHU
NKOSI SIKELELA
THINA LUSAPHO LWAYO

WOZA MOYA
(WOZA MOYA WOZA)
WOZA MOYA
(WOZA MOYA WOZA)
WOZA MOYA OYINGCWELE
NKOSI SIKELELA
THINA LUSAPHO LWAYO

GOD BLESS AFRICA
LET HER FAME RESOUND
HEAR OUR PRAYERS
GOD BLESS
WE ARE HER PEOPLE

COME SPIRIT
(COME SPIRIT COME)
COME SPIRIT
(COME SPIRIT COME)
COME HOLY SPIRIT
GOD BLESS
WE ARE HER PEOPLE

GOD BLESS AFRICA

SOUTH AFRICA'S NEW NATIONAL FLAG

WHITE

YELLOW

BLACK

RED

GREEN

BLUE

WHITE

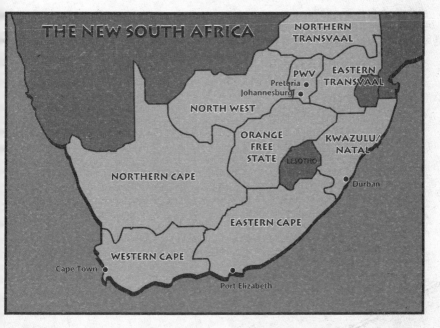

THE NEW SOUTH AFRICA

NORTHERN TRANSVAAL

PWV
Pretoria
Johannesburg

EASTERN TRANSVAAL

NORTH WEST

ORANGE FREE STATE

KWAZULU/ NATAL

LESOTHO

NORTHERN CAPE

Durban

EASTERN CAPE

WESTERN CAPE

Cape Town

Port Elizabeth

ACKNOWLEDGEMENTS My thanks to Roger Trask, Ursula Brown, Kieran Meeke, Mark Howe, Lou Bowker and Michal Boncza at Propeller Inc Ltd for their help; to Dave Pinchuck for faithfully supplying me with copies of the *Weekly Mail*; special thanks to Barbara McCrea for her support throughout the long, seemingly endless days of the project; and my deepest appreciation to Guy Berger for a stupendous effort and act true friendship in reading the manuscript at short notice and faxing copious pertinent comments in the final minutes of play.